SU
CO

TUBEROUS BEGONIAS

TUBEROUS BEGONIAS
An essential guide

JACK LARTER

THE CROWOOD PRESS

First published in 2011 by
The Crowood Press Ltd
Ramsbury, Marlborough
Wiltshire SN8 2HR

www.crowood.com

British Library Cataloguing-in-Publication Data
A catalogue record for this book is available from the British Library.

ISBN 978 1 84797 231 6

Front cover: 'Icemint' – a new introduction for 2007
Back cover: The winning twelve board at the National Show,
    Birmingham 2007
Frontispiece: The cut bloom classes at the National Show,
    Birmingham 2006

Typeset by Phoenix Typesetting, Auldgirth, Dumfriesshire
Printed and bound in India by Replika Press Pvt Ltd

Contents

Acknowledgements

To be successful in the pursuit of any hobby, you will need the help, advice and guidance from people who are already established in your chosen field. To that end I would like to thank my mentors both past and present.

I particularly thank Derek Telford and Dennis Hague for all the advice and photographs used in the chapter on growing pot plants.

I would also like to mention Cedric Ball who disrupted his greenhouse several times whilst we worked on the pendula (hanging basket) section.

Thanks also to Malcolm Watson for correcting my use of the English language and also for making valuable comments.

I cannot give enough thanks to Ron Knight without whose help this book would never have been written.

Finally, my thanks go to my wife Muriel who for years has welcomed my friends and visitors to our home, made endless cups of tea and coffee, and tolerated literally thousands of hours spent in my greenhouses growing these magnificent flowers.

Preface

I hope that you will find this book both interesting and helpful. If this proves to be the case then I will have achieved what I set out to do, that is, to get you interested enough to try growing a begonia or two.

It is my opinion that when a tuberous begonia is grown either as a pot plant or cut bloom and is shown at its best, then there is not another flower to equal it.

For me it all started when I was given a couple of tubers to grow, with the advice to 'go and grow a proper flower'. Well, I took that advice and did just that: I grew two 'proper' flowers. Those two flowers were magnificent and changed my life for ever. Little did I know at that time just how much it would change. I have two greenhouses; one door is labelled 'Paradise' and the other door is labelled 'Heaven'. These labels say it all.

I grow cut blooms for exhibiting and competing at shows. Not everybody wants to grow flowers for exhibiting; in my case it sort of just crept up on me. I had been visiting the shows at Huddersfield, Leeds and Southport with my mentors, watching what went on, totally mesmerized by the beautiful arrays of cut blooms, which were arranged in drinking cups on special wooden stands. I was encouraged and cajoled to try exhibiting in the novice sections, and eventually I made up my mind to have a try.

It is said that everyone is due a little luck in life. It was my luck to find not one but two begonia growers living quite close to me, and so began the slow job of gleaning every little piece of information on the cultivation of begonias from them. All this took place many years ago and if I am honest I am still learning and picking their brains to this day. I count myself fortunate to have had not only the opportunity to learn from them, but also the friendship that they have given to me over the years.

Jack Larter, 2010

CHAPTER 1

Tuberous begonias – growing and showing

About 1,500 separate species of begonia have been found so far growing wild in different parts of the tropical and subtropical world. The begonia genus is one of the largest in the plant kingdom and the different species can vary enormously.

Tuberous begonias are only one of the types of begonias in the genus. Other types of begonias include the fibrous rooted begonias; one type has been developed into the semperflorens begonias (*Begonia semperflorens*), which are very commonly used as half-hardy bedding plants. Another type are rhizomatous begonias; these include the *Begonia rex* hybrids with the spectacularly coloured leaves, often grown as houseplants.

TUBEROUS BEGONIAS

Tuberous begonias are so called because the plant forms a tuber at the base of the stem when the plant goes into dormancy during the winter period. The tuber acts as a storage organ that starts off the growth cycle in the following season.

Nowadays we think of tuberous begonias as the brilliant large double blooms seen at the summer flower shows, or the magnificent hanging baskets dripping with colour, or the fabulous bedding displays of Non Stop begonias in public parks, but these are the results of over a hundred years of hybridization. These modern varieties bear no relation to the small single flowered species of tuberous begonias that were originally selected for crossing and propagating.

Tuberous begonia flowers are now available in self-colours, bicolours and picotees of just about every shade from scarlet and crimson through to the palest of pinks, from bright orange and apricot through to pale peaches and buffs and from golden yellow through lemon to pale creams and pure whites. Unfortunately shades of blue have not yet been produced in begonia flowers.

GROWING

Growing tuberous begonias is easy. Seed or tubers can be bought quite cheaply from garden centres early in the year to be started off in a propagator. Or later on, plug plants and plantlets that have been started off by a commercial nursery can be purchased. These may be grown on in suitably sized pots or baskets, or planted out in the garden. Tuberous begonias have very few pests and diseases, and can be grown in sunny or shaded areas. So, provided the plants are kept frost-free and are watered when necessary, a colourful display should result, which will stay in bloom from early July until late September. Growing this way it is probably better to buy new stock the following year, rather than saving tubers over the winter period.

However, it is possible to do so much better. There are named varieties of tuberous begonias obtainable from specialist nurseries, for pot plants, for baskets and for outside bedding. These named varieties have been specially hybridized and selectively chosen to give bigger and more prolific blooms in a wide range of colours and colour combinations, capable of giving results incomparably better than the usual unnamed tubers and plants available at garden centres. Because these named varieties are the result of years of selective breeding and can only be propagated through cuttings, they

Begonia cinnabarina.

Begonia pearcei.

Three of the species that were originally hybridized and eventually produced the large double-flowered tuberous begonias that are grown today.

Begonia davisii.

are quite expensive to buy, so it is well worth learning how to grow them to get the best results, how to save the tubers for the following year, and how to propagate them to increase stock. This is the main purpose of this book.

SHOWING

The progression after growing these fabulous named varieties is often to move on to exhibiting the plants in competition at one of the summer flower shows.

At a show in the United Kingdom there are tuberous begonia classes for plants in pots, for plants in hanging baskets and for cut blooms. A cut bloom is the central male begonia flower cut from a plant grown in a pot in a greenhouse. These cut blooms are displayed in groups of three, six or twelve on specially constructed boards. Pot plants can be exhibited unrestricted, or restricted to one stem plus side shoots or one stem with no side shoots. These can be shown as single plants or in groups. Pendula begonias are always shown as single hanging baskets but there is no limit to the number of tubers in a basket.

Whether showing or not, this book explains how to grow cut blooms, pot plants and pendulas to exhibition standard.

CHAPTER 2

The greenhouse

A greenhouse full of begonias.

It is possible to grow some tuberous begonias without a greenhouse. Non Stop bedding begonia tubers could be started in an airing cupboard in March, grown on the windowsill until early June then planted outside. One or two of the large-flowered tuberous begonias could be started in the

airing cupboard and flowered on a windowsill but they would never reach their full potential. Growing and flowering in a conservatory would be better but even here the ideal requirements of shading and plenty of ventilation are difficult to maintain. The ideal place for growing tuberous begonias is in a dedicated greenhouse. This gives them the conditions they require to grow well and it is essential if growing for showing.

TYPES OF GREENHOUSE

There are many types of greenhouses, varying from huge Victorian constructions to the homemade greenhouse on the allotment made from old window frames and odds and ends, which can be made suitable for growing tuberous begonias.

If purchasing a greenhouse today the choice will probably be between a wooden-framed greenhouse and an aluminium-framed greenhouse. These can be fully glazed from floor to roof, or have half brick and half glazed sides. Glazing can be with glass, safety glass, polycarbonate or other plastics.

Wooden greenhouses have the advantage of being warmer and often more aesthetically pleasing but have the major disadvantage that the framework needs regular treatment with wood preserver to prevent rotting. This can be minimized if the framework is made from cedar wood, which is resistant to rotting. However, this makes it much more expensive. My own propagating greenhouse is a half brick, half wood construction which is easy to keep warm – the reason why my cuttings root so well.

Aluminium greenhouses have the advantage that the framework requires little or no maintenance. These are the most popular type of greenhouse and are available in a wide variety of styles and sizes. At extra cost they can be supplied powder-coated in various colours, which improves their appearance.

With both types of greenhouse it is easy to apply shading and easy to fix opening lights and side vents for ventilation. They are also easy to insulate with bubble-wrap or fleece. Both types of greenhouse are suitable for growing tuberous begonias.

A polytunnel or polyhouse can provide lots of space and light at a fraction of the cost of a glazed greenhouse. The disadvantages are that the plastic covering needs renewing every five years or so, and because of their appearance these are perhaps more suitable for an allotment. Ventilation can be a problem. The timber door frames at the ends of the polytunnel can be covered with netting, allowing ventilation without letting in insects or animals. With a greenhouse, the ventilation and cooling is achieved by hot air rising and escaping through the roof lights and so drawing in cooler air through the side vents. With a polytunnel the ventilation and cooling relies on a through draught from one end to the other (although some now have side openings). Provided there can be sufficient ventilation and shading there is no reason why polytunnels cannot be used for growing tuberous begonias successfully. If crop bars are fitted across the metal hoops, a polytunnel could be ideal for growing on baskets of pendula begonias, since these can take up a great deal of space in a conventional greenhouse.

One type of structure where ventilation is certainly not a problem is a shade house: a structure with a glazed and shaded roof and having at least three of the four sides consisting of mesh or shade nets. The glazed roof keeps the rain out and the mesh sides provide maximum ventilation and cooling and can keep out insects. These are the ideal conditions for growing tuberous begonias in the summer months. The disadvantage with a shade house is that it cannot be used for growing tuberous begonias whilst there is any danger of a frost. However, tuberous begonias can be started in a conventional greenhouse, then as they get bigger and all danger of frost has passed, they can be transferred to the shade house. With global warming and the likelihood of summers becoming warmer, a shade house becomes an attractive proposition.

BASES, FLOORING AND STAGING

If a new greenhouse is being erected, consideration must first be given to the type of base and floor that is to be used. Polyhouses and shade houses are normally erected on bare ground without a base, although a weed-inhibiting polypropylene sheeting to cover the entire area is advisable. With wooden or aluminium greenhouses some sort of base is necessary.

For smaller aluminium greenhouses, the simplest base is a galvanized steel structure purposely designed for the greenhouse, laid on bare level ground and anchored in concrete at each corner. For wooden or larger aluminium greenhouses, a brick or block base needs to be made; this must be accurately sized, square and level.

Before building a brick or block base it is best to

The staging in my greenhouse, made up of building blocks and wooden staging. The staging can be easily removed for cleaning.

decide what to do with the floor of the greenhouse. Some begonia growers prefer to have a bare earth floor claiming that this helps to keep the atmosphere cooler and more moist. Other begonia growers prefer concrete or flagged floors as they are easier to clean and sterilize. If the floor is to be bare earth the base can be built on footings (hardcore with concrete on top). Even with a bare earth floor it is still worthwhile having flagged paths and covering the earth with a weed-proof membrane with gravel on top. If a flagged or concrete floor is wanted then it is easier to prepare the floor and then build the base on top. Chippings or hardcore can be used as a base for flagstones or concrete. Thought needs to be given to any holes that will be required for electric cables, gas pipes, water pipes or drainage. Extra courses of bricks or blocks, if this can be done, will give more headroom to the greenhouse and will make it easier to keep cool in the summer months.

Large-flowered tuberous begonias can be grown on the floor of a greenhouse and in some ways this can be advantageous as it is cooler at floor level and there will be less damage if a pot topples over. However, begonia flowers are best viewed and inspected at somewhere near eye level, so some sort of staging is preferable.

Staging is usually made from wood or aluminium but galvanized mesh can also be used. To aid air circulation, slatted or meshed staging is preferred to solid-topped benches. Wooden staging has the advantage that the average handyman can build the staging to the size and shapes required, perhaps using concrete blocks as supports, and this will be much cheaper than buying aluminium staging from a manufacturer. The disadvantage of wood is that it needs to be protected with a wood preserver and ideally painted with a wood stain, unless it is cedar wood, which does not need protecting. Aluminium staging requires no maintenance but it can be very expensive to kit out a whole greenhouse. With any kind of staging it is a benefit if it can be easily dismantled at the end of the season so that the inside of the greenhouse can be thoroughly cleaned and disinfected.

Tuberous begonias that are to be grown for cut bloom exhibition or pot plants with a single stem and no side shoots are best grown on tiered staging. All the blooms are then easy to see and examine, and watering the pots is easier. These begonias will probably be finally grown in 7in or 8in (3 or 4 litre) pots, so the tiers need to be at least 12in (30cm) wide with at least 6in (15cm) in height between the tiers. The number of tiers possible depends on the size of the greenhouse, but there should be no more than three or it will not be possible to reach the back tier.

Multi-stemmed pot plant begonias take up a lot of room, so these will need to be grown on a slatted bench. The space under staging should not be wasted. It can be very useful to grow on begonia cuttings and the drips of water from above do not seem to cause any harm.

SHADING AND VENTILATION

Shading and ventilation of the greenhouse to reduce temperatures during the summer months are essential for the successful growing of large-flowered tuberous begonias. Strong sunshine through glass will certainly cause leaf scorch, particularly if there has been any water spilled on the leaves during watering. Overheating because of lack of ventilation will make begonias wilt and if short of water they will die. Keeping temperatures lower slows down the development of the bud to bloom, which seems to give bigger blooms that last longer before going past their best. Ventilation and circulation of air also reduces the chances of fungal infections such as mildew.

Shading should not be too dense. A bright diffused light inside the greenhouse is ideal. The amount of light affects the colour of the blooms, more shading tending to give duller blooms. Shading should be applied in April, possibly increased in midsummer, and removed in October. It should be applied to the roof and walls, particularly the south wall, of the greenhouse.

There are various shading materials that can be applied to the outside of the greenhouse. Proprietary materials include white powders that are dispersed in water and liquid materials which act as a shading when dry but become translucent when wet. White emulsion paint can be used diluted 1:1 with water. The paint should be the cheapest available, as this will be more easily removed at the end of the season. All these materials can be applied by brush or sprayed on. A long-handled paint roller is ideal for reaching across the roof of the greenhouse.

Various grades of netting can also be used as shading and different types of blinds are available for either inside or outside the greenhouse. Inside the greenhouse fitted roller blinds, horticultural fleece or thermal screening can be used as shading and these will also give some degree of insulation.

When outside temperatures allow, roof windows, side windows and louvre vents should be left open to give maximum ventilation. Automatic openers can be very useful if the greenhouse cannot be attended to during the day. At the height of summer if there is insufficient ventilation, panes of glass can be removed from the sides of the greenhouse. If growing for exhibition, insect mesh should be fitted to all the openings to prevent moths, earwigs and other flying insects from causing damage.

In hot weather it is beneficial to damp down the floor, which cools the greenhouse, and also creates humidity, which the begonias will appreciate.

The effect of light

Without light, plant growth is not possible. Light supplies the energy to convert carbon dioxide and water by photosynthesis into carbohydrate and oxygen. Different plants have different requirements for light; some can be either shade loving or sun loving.

Tuberous begonias grown outside prefer semi-shade to full sun, and along with *Impatiens*, are the preferred bedding plants for shady areas of the garden. However, tuberous begonias will still give a good display in a sunny area and are very rarely affected by sun scorch.

In the greenhouse if a tuberous begonia does not get enough light, the plant becomes drawn with paler green leaves. In the greenhouse the effect of too much sunlight becomes difficult to determine because it is hard to separate the effects of too much light and too much heat. Increased amounts of light will make the plant grow squatter with thicker stems, but unless the greenhouse is shaded the increased heat from the sunlight will cause the leaves to scorch. Most growers consider it essential to shade the greenhouse in the summer months between April and October. The increased heat also makes the begonias grow more quickly so the plants flower more quickly and have smaller blooms, and the blooms do not last as long. In more northern parts of the UK, the intensity of the sunshine is less, giving fewer heat problems, but the daylight hours are longer in the summer months. Perhaps this is why the Scottish begonia growers are renowned for the size of their begonia blooms.

It is the effect of light on the colour of blooms that is most interesting. Some varieties of tuberous begonias, when compared growing in shady or sunny situations, could be mistaken for two quite distinct varieties. In general, strong bright shades such as reds and oranges will be much brighter when grown in good light and can be rather insipid and pale when grown in poor light. Pale pastel shades, however, need to be grown in poorer light, because in brighter light they often show some blotchiness or a nuance in colour and tend to fade. On this basis it might be thought that picotee colours should be grown in a more shaded position, but it is found that growing in a better light will give a stronger picotee edge to a bloom with less bleeding.

The type of light that the blooms are viewed in also has an effect on the colour of the blooms. Viewing begonia blooms at night in the greenhouse under the warm glow of a standard electric light bulb takes some beating. Some flower shows are held indoors with fluorescent lighting and this can have weird effects on the bloom colour. The best place to have a flower show is in a marquee with no artificial light.

There are artificial lights that can be used to enhance natural light at the beginning of the season or to extend the season for taking cuttings. These must be genuine growing lights. It is important that they emit the correct wavelengths of light which can be utilized by the plants, and that the directions are followed in positioning the bulbs to give the correct intensity of light.

There is one area where absence of light is important and that is with the root growth. As root growth shies away from the light, there is a trick that can be used when growing single-stem plants to make full use of all the compost in the pot. By placing pieces of thin slate to cover the surface of the compost and hiding the light, it will be found that roots will completely fill the compost. The slates will also stop 'cratering' when watering, although it will be more difficult to tell when watering is needed.

HEATING AND INSULATION

To start tubers into growth in February or March, a temperature of around 20°C (68°F) is required and ideally this will be provided by a hot bed or a propagator. Once tubers have started into growth and have been potted up, some form of heating will be required early in the season to ensure that night-time temperatures do not fall below 10°C (50°F), which will check growth. Whilst the tubers are in small pots it may not be necessary to heat the whole greenhouse: a small part can be sectioned off with insulated partitions. At the end of the season, from October onwards, some heat will be required to prevent frost damage to plants and cuttings until the tubers can be put away for the winter. Any late cuttings may need to be grown on through the winter and are best placed on the hot bed or brought into the house to reduce heating costs.

The most convenient method of heating and temperature control for a greenhouse is an electric fan heater with a remote thermostat. This method has the added advantage of circulating the air, which gives a more even temperature throughout the greenhouse and also reduces the chance of mildew attacking the begonias. The in-built fan without the heat can also be used to circulate air in the summer months. Electricity supply to a greenhouse must be installed by a qualified electrician.

If an electricity supply is not available to the greenhouse then paraffin heaters, Calor gas heaters or even natural gas heaters can be used. Whatever method of heating is used it is important that the heater is powerful enough for the size of the greenhouse. A maximum and minimum thermometer should be provided to see what temperatures are achieved. Traditionally, a hot water system of 4in (10cm) cast-iron pipes fed from a boiler fuelled by gas, oil or solid fuel was the optimum system, and has been employed by generations of career horticulturists.

Insulation of the roof and walls will keep the greenhouse warmer in the cooler months and reduce heating bills. The insulation should be applied in October and can be kept on until the following April. Double-sided 1in (25mm) bubble insulation is best for retaining heat in the greenhouse but it can be a bit awkward to put up, it takes up a lot of storage space when not in use, and it only lasts two or three years. Horticultural fleece, as well as shading the greenhouse, will also act as an insulator.

MAKING A THERMOSTATICALLY CONTROLLED HEATED PROPAGATING BENCH

Although not absolutely essential, a thermostatically controlled heated propagating bench – another name for a hot box, or (if it is fitted with a lid) a heated propagator – is an extremely useful piece of equipment for the begonia grower:

- It can be used for starting off tubers, both cutting tubers and adult tubers, giving the constant even temperature that begonias require. The tubers can be started off in trays or pots, or in a layer of compost in the hot box.
- It can be used for propagating cuttings where the gentle bottom heat will encourage the cuttings to root more quickly.
- It can be used to give a boost to ailing plants.
- It can be used for drying off tubers at the end of the season. By inverting a few empty plant pots and laying a sheet of fine galvanized mesh on top, a simple support on which to lay the tubers is easily assembled. The gentle bottom heat will help to dry the tubers. With the

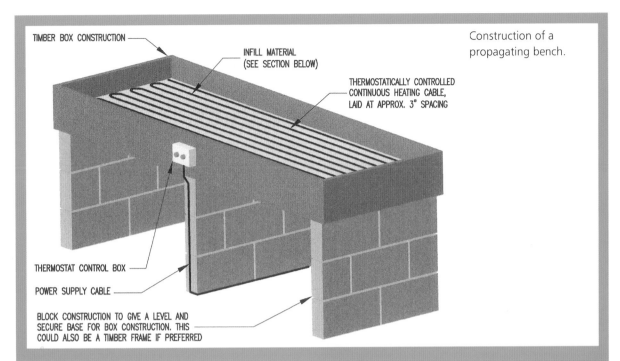

TIMBER BOX CONSTRUCTION

INFILL MATERIAL
(SEE SECTION BELOW)

THERMOSTATICALLY CONTROLLED
CONTINUOUS HEATING CABLE,
LAID AT APPROX. 3" SPACING

THERMOSTAT CONTROL BOX

POWER SUPPLY CABLE

BLOCK CONSTRUCTION TO GIVE A LEVEL AND
SECURE BASE FOR BOX CONSTRUCTION. THIS
COULD ALSO BE A TIMBER FRAME IF PREFERRED

Construction of a
propagating bench.

heating turned down low it is possible to overwinter the tubers in the hot box, with a gentle heat circulating to keep them in prime condition.

The description below is of a tried and tested propagating bench that has been in use for many years. The area dimensions can be made to suit particular requirements. It must be remembered that a propagating bench full of wet sand is extremely heavy, so it needs to be on a firm foundation such as a flagged or concrete floor or concrete footings. The bench also needs to be level.

The bench is constructed inside the greenhouse, across the end or along one side, where an electricity supply is available. (If it is necessary to install electricity to the greenhouse, a qualified electrician must be employed.)

The wooden base of the bench is 18mm plywood, strengthened by battens. The sides of the box are tongue and groove timber. The base of the box is insulated with 25mm polystyrene sheet. The waterproof layer is pond liner material. Builders' sharp sand is used. If there is a problem laying out the heating cable correctly, it can be tied to a wire mesh and the whole thing buried in the sand layer.

A simple lid for the hot box.

The sand through which the heated cable is laid should never dry out. As an alternative to having one long heating cable, it may be preferable to have two shorter cables with two thermostats, so that if required a smaller area can be heated. Every two or three years, the heated cable should be removed, checked for any damage and renewed if necessary.

If a lid is required to allow the hot box to be used as a propagator, it can be cheaply and easily made from PVC extrusions, cut and glued together with superglue and covered with thick-gauge polythene sheeting.

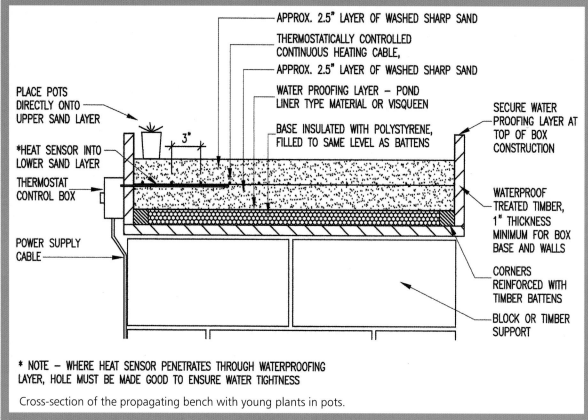

APPROX. 2.5" LAYER OF WASHED SHARP SAND

THERMOSTATICALLY CONTROLLED
CONTINUOUS HEATING CABLE,

APPROX. 2.5" LAYER OF WASHED SHARP SAND

WATER PROOFING LAYER – POND
LINER TYPE MATERIAL OR VISQUEEN

BASE INSULATED WITH POLYSTYRENE,
FILLED TO SAME LEVEL AS BATTENS

PLACE POTS
DIRECTLY ONTO
UPPER SAND LAYER

3"

*HEAT SENSOR INTO
LOWER SAND LAYER

THERMOSTAT
CONTROL BOX

POWER SUPPLY
CABLE

SECURE WATER
PROOFING LAYER AT
TOP OF BOX
CONSTRUCTION

WATERPROOF
TREATED TIMBER,
1" THICKNESS
MINIMUM FOR BOX
BASE AND WALLS

CORNERS
REINFORCED WITH
TIMBER BATTENS

BLOCK OR TIMBER
SUPPORT

* NOTE – WHERE HEAT SENSOR PENETRATES THROUGH WATERPROOFING
LAYER, HOLE MUST BE MADE GOOD TO ENSURE WATER TIGHTNESS

Cross-section of the propagating bench with young plants in pots.

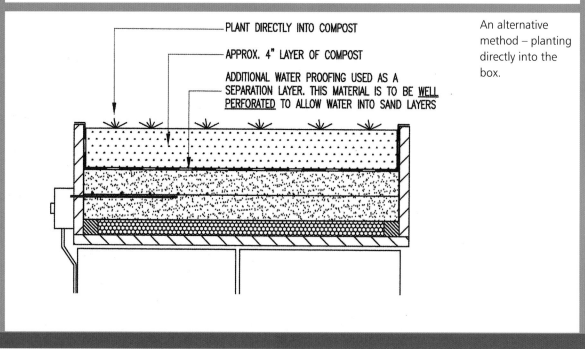

PLANT DIRECTLY INTO COMPOST

APPROX. 4" LAYER OF COMPOST

ADDITIONAL WATER PROOFING USED AS A
SEPARATION LAYER. THIS MATERIAL IS TO BE <u>WELL
PERFORATED</u> TO ALLOW WATER INTO SAND LAYERS

An alternative
method – planting
directly into the
box.

MY GREENHOUSE THROUGHOUT THE SEASONS

Second week in April

The cutting tubers that were started off in January are now potted up and spaced out in my large greenhouse. No heating is being used but heating is there if required. Note that there is no debris or mess of any kind on the floor. The Agrifleece is already in place. The slatted shelves were scrubbed with Jeyes Fluid prior to being placed in the greenhouse. If you keep your greenhouse clean you will have fewer problems throughout the year.

First week in June

The cutting tubers that were in this greenhouse have been placed outside and now the adult tubers that were started off in March have taken their place. These plants will soon need to have support canes placed into the pots. Once the adults are in their final pots, with the canes in place, there is a quiet period when the plants just seem to grow. They require foliar feeding and their flower buds need to be removed. Watch your leaves for any yellowing: this can mean that the plant is too wet or a feed with a nitrogen fertilizer is required.

First week in August

I grow cut blooms for exhibition and so have introduced the polystyrene plates by this stage. The plates are mainly used to stop any damage to the buds by leaves and clumsy fingers. The plates also help to shield the blooms from the heat of the sun – but remember polystyrene can also get warm and outer petals can stick to them. The plates are also useful in estimating the size of the final blooms.

The flower buds were selected when the buds were 1⅛in or 30mm in diameter. Once the flower bud was chosen, the plant was stopped by removing the growing tip. This allows all the energy to go into the bloom. Different varieties vary in the time that the blooms take to open. It is important to make notes of the number of days the different varieties take to open, so that you can make adjustments the following year.

One of my mentors used to tell me leaves should be the colour of a good privet hedge and so that is what I aim for. Your leaves will give you advance warning when things are not quite to their liking by showing yellowing, spotting, mottling, scorching or limpness. Problems are the last thing you want in a greenhouse

full of plants, so when nature gives you a warning via the leaves, try to sort it immediately. Over-watering, under-watering, limp leaves can all be corrected provided they are not left too long. Remember that giving a plant a good feed of nitrogen does not cure all ills and pumping food into a plant will not give you a good bloom. Too much feeding produces a lot of foliage to the detriment of the flowers. To obtain the beautiful blooms you desire you first have to build a good strong plant. The 'psychology' of plants is that they flower to produce seed in order to propagate the species. A well-fed plant does not feel threatened and so does not need to flower for seed so urgently. I have found that if your compost is right, you pot up correctly, and water properly, you will not need to feed very much at all.

Third week in August

As you can see there are too many plants in the greenhouse. This is the time of the year when I start to select which blooms have a chance of making it to the show. Having made my selections, the unselected ones go outside into the garden for everyone to enjoy.

As the days go by other faults start to appear. It is at this time of the year that the begonia exhibitor really starts to worry. Blooms that are showing brown marks on the petal edges (edging), or have insect damage, blotching or colour-run, join those plants already outside. So my chosen plants gradually get fewer and fewer and in turn enjoy the extra space. There is less and less choice, certain varieties are no longer an option, and so it goes on, but with any luck I will see you at the showground!

First week in October

All the begonias have now been brought in from outside and are packed in wherever I can put them. The Agrifleece is still in place. The stand that you can see at the back of the greenhouse is a platform that can be rotated, making it possible to inspect a plant from all angles.

Watering of the adult tubers was gradually reduced from mid-September and eventually stopped in early October. You can see that some of the leaves are just starting to turn yellow. They will eventually fall off as the plant continues to die back. This is the time of year when mildew will start to show. It does no harm at all to give a preventive spray of fungicide. The important thing at this time of year is to remove all fallen leaves and other debris before botrytis sets in.

Third week in October

The adult tubers are drying out. They will drop their stems and will be harvested in November. Allow the stems to detach naturally; try to resist the temptation to waggle the stems, as they will come off when they are ready. The cuttings will take longer to decline because I have continued to water them until now, but from now they will get no more water. They will still continue to absorb moisture from the air through their leaves, swelling the small tuber that should have formed. These small tubers are the future, so we must give them every opportunity to develop.

The dormant season

When the greenhouse is empty of plants and the tubers are cleaned and packed away for the winter dormancy, the important business of cleaning and sterilization the greenhouse begins.

The greenhouse staging has been constructed so that it can all be taken down and moved outside where it can be scrubbed clean with a hard brush using greenhouse disinfectant. This is then washed off using a pressure hose. The inside of the greenhouse is stripped of the fleece, to be washed in the washing machine on a soft wash. By this means the fleece should last for two seasons.

The inside and outside of the greenhouse get the same treatment: washing with the disinfectant and hosing down with the pressure hose. Particular care is taken to clean the sheets of glass where they overlap. Once the glass has been cleaned the flagged floor is scrubbed down thoroughly and the staging moved back in. The greenhouse is now left open so that the frost can get in and see off any bugs that have been missed.

When February comes around, fumigate the greenhouse before any plants are put in. I use a couple tins of sulphur obtained from the garden centre (check your greenhouse size against the instructions on the tin to see how many tins are required). Fumigating should be done when there is no wind, with all the windows and vents closed. If you have a metal heater or fan in the greenhouse, this should be removed because sulphur will tarnish any shiny metal screws and fittings. After lighting the wicks, quickly withdraw from the greenhouse and close the door. Leave overnight. The fumes will do the rest, wafting into every nook and cranny destroying insects, insect eggs and fungal spores. In the morning the doors can be opened to dissipate any remaining fumes.

The greenhouse is now ready for the new season of growing begonias.

SOME USEFUL PRODUCTS

A range of useful products.

Back row (left to right): Jeyes Fluid (powerful disinfectant), Chempak Foliar Feed, Provado bug killer (spray), Miracle-Gro plant food, Bio Fillip Foliar Feed, green sulphur powder, Chempak No 2 (high nitrogen feed), Chempak No 4 (high potash feed). Middle row (left to right): Provado vine weevil killer, methylated spirit (for sterilizing wounds), Systhane (fungicide), yellow sulphur, Nimrod T (fungicide), Provado bug killer (effective for six weeks), Maxicrop Take Root (enhances root growth), sulphur candle (for sterilizing the greenhouse). Front (left to right): plant labels, cotton wool buds (for removing dross and insects from blooms), Murphys hormone rooting powder, green nylon twine, craft knife and blades, flitch brushes (for applying sulphur), small pointed scissors.

Some useful equipment.

CHAPTER 3

Growing

And so to the growing of begonias. Tuberous begonias are not difficult to grow. Buying a tuber and growing it frost-free in any kind of commercial compost will usually give a good colourful display of blooms during the summer months. However, to grow well, up to exhibition standard, and propagate and keep expensive named varieties year after year requires a lot more care and thought. My approach is detailed below; other begonia growers may have slightly different methods.

Tuberous begonias can be grown either from seed or from tubers. Growing from seed should give many more plants for the money, but if growing from tubers, results are virtually guaranteed to be successful. Seeds of different types of tuberous begonias are available from most seed merchants. It is also possible to purchase plug plants, where the germination and initial thinning out has already been done by the supplier. Begonia tubers can be purchased from most garden centres in early spring for a very modest sum and there is nothing wrong with these tubers for general garden use. However, to grow these beautiful plants and see them at their very best, it is better to purchase some named variety tubers from a specialist commercial grower. These tubers will certainly cost more money, but the quality of the blooms is far superior.

GROWING FROM SEED

Seed for Non Stop bedding begonias is widely available. Seed for large-flowered begonias should be obtained from a specialist commercial nursery. To see the blooms from seed in the same year as it is sown, seed needs to be sown in January, in a propagator, in the greenhouse where the temperature can be maintained and monitored.

Growing from seed needs a plan of action something like this:

- Take a clean seed pan or a 5in or 6in (12.5cm or 15cm) half pot, well crocked in the bottom inch or so. Cover the crock with ¾in (2cm) of ⅛in (3mm) washed grit.
- Add well-sieved seed compost and very lightly firm down.
- Place the seed pan or half pot in a saucer of water. The water is drawn up through the crock and grit and when the surface of the compost changes colour it is wet enough.
- Begonia seed is extremely fine and for the best results must be sown thinly. Adding a small amount of silver sand to the seed before sprinkling over the surface of the compost will help to give an even distribution.
- Very gently, firm the seed on to the compost.
- Cover the seed pan with a piece of glass and place into the hot bed where the temperature is maintained at around 68°F (20°C).

There is nothing that can be done now but wait for the seeds to grow. Ensure the compost never dries out or the seed will be lost. Check the seed and wipe off the drops of condensation which form underneath the glass so that they do not drop on to the germinating seed.

In approximately two weeks time the seed should have started to germinate and it will first appear as a green shadow. As the days go by the single tiny leaves will soon become two. The glass over the seed pan can now be raised slightly so that the minute seedlings can get accustomed to the ambient greenhouse temperature. The glass can be removed completely in a day or two. Cheshunt compound

Begonia seed is notoriously slow to germinate and grow.

can be added to the water being used to help prevent the seedlings from damping off and fungus from forming.

As soon as the seedlings are large enough they will need pricking out into seed trays where they can be grown on. A plant label which has a V cut into the end is very handy when pricking out begonia seedlings. Begonias are not the fastest growers, but they will need to be potted on and given space to develop as soon as it is necessary.

If the seedlings are the Non Stop type of begonia for outside bedding, they need to be hardened off in

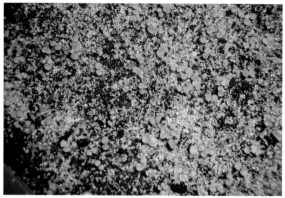

The seed has germinated successfully and is growing nicely. Note that the glass cover has now been removed. The seedlings are now at greenhouse temperature. It is fairly certain that more seedlings will poke their heads through in due course.

the cold frame before planting out when all danger of frost has passed. Seedlings of large-flowered double begonias need to be kept in the greenhouse for longer.

Provided they have been given care and attention, there should be some very nice begonia flowers to enjoy later in the year. At the end of the season the tubers can be lifted, dried and stored ready for the next year as described below in 'Growing from adult tubers'. Do not keep any inferior plants. The Non Stop begonia tubers can be grown on for two or three years; when the tubers get too big it is easier to grow new plants from fresh seed.

One last point worth mentioning about growing from seed is hybridization. To obtain new varieties, selected plants are cross-pollinated and hundreds of seedlings are grown in the hope that there may be one with an improvement over the current varieties. Hybridization is discussed more fully in Chapter 10.

GROWING FROM CUTTING TUBERS

Cutting tubers are the result of the cuttings taken from plants the previous year. If the cuttings were taken correctly and looked after properly, the reward will be a mixture of assorted sized tubers, from pea size to walnut size, harvested at the end of the year.

These cutting tubers need a resting time before starting back into growth, generally around three or four weeks is fine. Any longer is likely to result in the smaller cutting tubers drying out and becoming hard and possibly rotting when planted up. I find the best way of storing them in the rest period is to lay them in a tray, cover with coir and keep cool but frost free.

Prior to starting either adult or cutting tubers it is worthwhile giving them a dip in a 10 per cent domestic bleach solution, (1 part bleach to 9 parts tepid water), making sure that you use rubber gloves when handling bleach. The tubers are placed into the solution and left for 15 minutes, after which they are removed and rinsed off in clean water. There are two reasons for treating tubers with bleach solution: firstly, it completely cleans them of any bugs or fungi; secondly, it enables the tuber to start to take

Cutting tubers being rinsed in clean water after having been dipped in bleach solution.

The smaller of the cutting tubers have now been planted. Notice the tops are just proud of the surface of the compost.

up water, giving it a kick start when planted in the hot bed or propagator.

Towards the end of January or the beginning of February, after the treatment with bleach solution, the cutting tubers are planted up. I use peat mixed with a small amount of seed fertilizer to which I add about 40 per cent of perlite. This makes a very open mix, friable and pleasant to handle. The small cutting tubers are planted into trays with the tops just peeking through the compost so that if there is any sign of fungus or rot it can be seen and the offending tuber can be dealt with. The next step is to water lightly and place the trays on the heated propagating bench (hot bed) or a commercial propagator (preferably with variable temperature control) – or even a windowsill in a warm room. Try to maintain a temperature of 68°F (20°C). The growing season has begun.

There can be considerable variation in the time for the signs of growth to be noticed with the different cutting tubers, anything from two to six

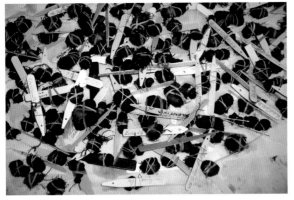

Tubers drying out after being in the bleach treatment.

weeks. If any of the cutting tubers are taking longer they should be checked for rot.

It will not be very long (when the shoots are about 2in or 5cm high) before the cutting tubers will need to be removed from the trays and put in their first pot. I use a multi-purpose compost with about 20 per cent added coarse grit or perlite to aid drainage for the first potting. The size of the root ball determines the size of the plant pot. I like to pot small so I choose a pot that will take the root ball plus ¾in (2cm) all round. Put about an inch (2–3cm) of compost into the pot, place the root ball onto the compost and fill round it, ensuring that the top of the tuber is covered with compost. Give a gentle tap or two to firm the compost around the roots, and

The cutting tubers are starting to produce pips, and the small cutting tubers are starting into life. Not all cutting tubers show pips early. Some start off by growing their roots and the first indication of this is when you start to notice the roots running along the surface of the compost. The pips will follow when the plant is ready.

Cutting tubers starting to form their first leaves.

At the end of the season the cutting tubers are drying off nicely.

finally water lightly. The potted up cutting tubers are kept in the greenhouse at this time of the year and some heating will be necessary if the temperature is forecast to fall below 50°F (10°C). The begonia cutting tuber has begun its adult life.

These cutting tubers are not big enough to produce a multi-stemmed pot plant in this first season. Keen exhibitors of cut blooms often prefer to flower on two-year or older tubers. If it is not intended to flower, the cutting tubers can stay in this first pot for the whole of the season, just getting watered and fed occasionally. When all danger of frost is past, these cutting tubers in their pots are placed outside for the remainder of the season, in my case underneath the berberis hedge in the front garden. Cuttings can be taken from these cutting tuber plants. Flower buds should be removed as soon as they appear, and the plants stopped by pinching out the growing tips when they get top heavy. The reason for removing buds and pinching out the growing tips is to ensure that all the energy the plants make this season will go into making the tubers bigger so that in the following season they should give bigger and better flowers.

If it is intended to flower the cutting tubers, then they will make a decent single-stem pot plant or even a reasonable cut bloom and they should be grown as

This cutting tuber is ready for its first pot. Note the root ball.

When the stems drop off, the cutting tubers can be harvested.

described in Chapters 4 and 5. At the end of the season, however, the tuber will be smaller than if it hadn't been allowed to flower. It is not possible to have both a large flower and a large tuber.

At the end of the season these tubers are lifted, dried and stored ready for the next year, as described below in 'Growing from adult tubers'.

GROWING FROM ADULT TUBERS

Adult tubers, here meaning tubers at least two years old, are generally started in the period from early February to early April. Multi-stemmed pot plants and pendula varieties need to be started earlier giving more time to grow into a bigger plant. The middle of March is a good time to start cut bloom and other single-stem begonias, as by this time there will be space in the propagator or hot bed because the cutting tubers will have been taken out and potted up. Tubers started in the middle of March should produce plants that will flower from early July all the way through August and well into September. Flower shows for begonias always take place between the middle of July and early September. Tuber starting dates may be varied slightly in different parts of the UK depending on the climate. With possible climate change in the future, tuber starting dates may have to be altered.

There are two different pre-treatments that can be done to adult tubers before starting them off. Neither of the pre-treatments is essential but some growers think that one or other is beneficial to the growth of the tubers. The first pre-treatment is the bleach treatment exactly as described above in 'Growing from cutting tubers'. This cleans the tubers of any bugs or fungi. The other pre-treatment is what is called the 'hot water treatment'. The hot water treatment was originally developed to kill any eelworms that may be nestling in the over-wintered tubers. With the use of sterilized compost, eelworm is rarely encountered, so this treatment is no longer necessary for this purpose. However, many growers feel that the hot water treatment helps to plump up the tubers and gets them starting earlier with more shoots developing. The hot water treatment involves immersing the tubers in hot water at a temperature of 115°F (46°C), no hotter, for a period of 15 to 20 minutes, after which the tubers are removed and plunged into cold water for a further 15 minutes. What I do with my adult tubers is slightly different. I do the bleach treatment, but at the end of the growing season, and allow the tubers to dry off before storing them away for the winter period. I only do the hot water pre-treatment on tubers that are particularly dry or if I have obtained tubers from an unknown source.

The adult tubers are now planted up. I use a 50:50 mix of multi-purpose compost and perlite, and plant directly into the hot bed, but a propagator can be used. The tubers should be completely covered with compost, as roots will come from all over the tuber. It can take as long as six weeks before the new shoots will emerge through the compost. This is a very exciting time and I am always on the lookout for new shoots appearing. Some tubers will produce several shoots. These tubers may be used to grow multi-stemmed pot plants. If growing for single stem plants, either for pot plants or cut blooms, wait until the shoots are about 3in (7.5cm) high, remove the weaker shoots and use as cuttings. These are basal cuttings and this is a very good way of increasing stock.

It is about this time, when the shoots are about 3in (7.5cm) in height, that the tubers should be moved to their first pot, taking great care not to break any of the new root system. Remove the tuber with the root ball from the hot bed and select a pot approximately 1in (2.5cm) all round larger than the root ball for this first potting. I use a peat-based compost to ensure that the plant gets a good start in life, because the root system will travel through a soft medium

Plants in the hot bed ready for the first potting.

GROWING MEDIA

The two main types of compost available to the amateur grower are soil-less composts made from peat, to which fertilizers and other materials are added, and soil-based composts such as the John Innes range. Both types of compost are based on sterilized ingredients; this helps to eradicate diseases and pests such as nematodes. Mixtures of the two types of compost are also available.

The soil-less composts are made from sphagnum moss peat or sedge peat, incorporating fertilizers and often additives such as sand, perlite, vermiculite, wetting agents and growth promoters. These types of compost are termed 'multipurpose composts', as the one compost is claimed to be suitable for all uses from planting seeds to potting on shrubs. As there is no set formula for multipurpose composts, their suitability for growing begonias can vary enormously.

The soil-based John Innes composts are made to a set formula developed during the Second World War, and so there is much less variation between different suppliers. There are different John Innes composts for different purposes. John Innes No 1 compost has the least fertilizer and can be used for sowing seeds and striking or rooting cuttings. John Innes No 2 compost has extra fertilizer and can be used to pot up seedlings and rooted cuttings. John Innes No 3 compost has even more fertilizer and is used when a plant is to stay in a pot for a longer period. All the John Innes composts are made up from the same base mixture of 7 parts sterilized loam + 3 parts peat + 2 parts horticultural sand (parts are by volume).

The fertilizer amounts to add to make 1 bushel (8 imperial gallons) of the John Innes Potting Composts are:

Potting Compost	Hoof and Horn*	Super phosphate	Sulphate of Potash	Chalk or Limestone**
J.I. No 1	1½ oz	1½ oz	¾ oz	¾ oz
J.I. No 2	3 oz	3 oz	1½ oz	1½ oz
J.I. No 3	4½ oz	4½ oz	2¼ oz	2¼ oz

* Good quality hoof and horn is now difficult to source. Some manufacturers are substituting with other material.
** Variable depending on the pH value of the loam. Loam can vary from different parts of the country:

in some areas the loam is of a fine texture and quite friable, and in other areas it is hard and lumpy and can be almost solid clay. Loam can have different colours due to the chemical make-up in the soil of the region. The majority of loams can be used to produce compost, but the pH values can vary.

There are differences between the two types of compost when it comes to growing tuberous begonias:

- The physical differences. Multipurpose compost is mainly peat so has a light, fluffy consistency, whereas soil-based composts are much heavier and more compact. Fully grown pot plants can have a tendency to topple over, and heavier compost will help prevent this. Some growers add grit to their compost. As well as improving drainage this increases weight to help stabilize the plant pot.
- There is a difference in how the two types of compost take up water. More care needs to be taken with watering multipurpose compost because it tends to dry out more quickly. If a pot containing peat-based multipurpose compost dries out, it is very difficult to wet it again. This problem does not occur with soil-based composts. Some of the multipurpose composts are formulated with wetting agents to help overcome this problem.
- The main difference between the two types of compost, however, is in the effect it has on

A bushel box, made to measure one bushel. The inside measurements are 22in×10in×10in (56cm×25cm×25cm).

the root formation of the tuberous begonias. With peat-based multipurpose compost, plant growth and root growth is much quicker than in soil-based compost, and the roots can be thick and creamy white with red tips. With soil-based compost, plant growth and root growth are much slower and the roots are very fine and darker than roots grown in multipurpose compost. Because of the slower root growth, when potting on with soil-based compost, the new pot should be no more than 1in (2.5cm) bigger all round to avoid getting sour compost. With peat-based composts it is possible to pot on at up to 2in (5cm) all round.

Both types of compost will produce strong plants with good big blooms. Some growers think that growing in a soil-based compost, such as John Innes No 2, gives slightly bigger blooms with slightly more depth because the flowers take longer to develop, and possibly they stay fresher a little longer before edging. Some growers use a 50:50 mixture of the two types of compost, hoping to get the best of both worlds. I myself start off my tubers in multipurpose compost to get the rapid root growth and early cuttings, and then I pot on into soil-based John Innes No 2 compost. Whatever sort of growing media you decide to grow in, if it works well for you, stick to it and if you decide to experiment start on one or two plants only.

Whichever compost is preferred, it should have been stored undercover so that it is dry when purchased and the nutrients have not been leached away. It is not always possible to tell, but purchased compost should also be fresh. Some of the nutrients can break down over prolonged storage. The quality of different manufacturers' composts does vary considerably. There are some really good peat-based and soil-based products available and it is worth asking other growers which compost they use.

An alternative is to make your own compost. The formulations for John Innes composts are free to use. Sterilized loam can be purchased along with the other ingredients. A base fertilizer plus trace elements is available, and the whole lot can be thoroughly mixed together, turning over at least three times. To make a type of multipurpose compost, there are different sorts of peat originating from different countries, which can be bought and mixed with fertilizer. The big advantage of making your own compost is that you know that it is fresh and that the nutrients will last around 4 to 6 weeks before further feeding is required.

Horticultural peat is sourced from renewable bogs and is usually advertised as such on the bales. There is pressure to reduce, or eliminate, the use of peat and peat-free composts are already available. Coir dust made from coconut fibre is being successfully used in propagating begonia cuttings. Whether it can grow a tuberous begonia to show bench standard is still to be seen. Possibly the use of finely shredded wood chippings and bark will also play a part in the growing mediums of the future. Other countries seem to manage without peat.

The make-up of commercial composts is likely to change in the near future. There is pressure from the UK Government for a percentage of composted green recycled council waste to be incorporated into all commercial growing media and this is already happening in some brands.

It is certainly worthwhile recycling the compost that has been used to grow your begonias. Just as it comes out of the pot it is excellent mulch for the borders in the garden. Riddled to remove some of the lumps and roots, it makes an excellent top dressing for the lawn or with a bit of fertilizer added it can be used in containers for hardy or half-hardy annuals.

---

more quickly than through a harder one. The plants are grown on in the greenhouse but the temperature should not be allowed to fall below 50°F (10°C).

For the next and subsequent pottings I use a loam based compost, John Innes No 2, which gives slower root growth than a peat-based compost but allows the plant a longer time to develop, culminating in better quality blooms. Always be aware that with a John Innes compost, when repotting, increase the size of the pot by no more than 1in (2.5cm) so that the compost does not go sour. If a peat-based compost is used, potting can be done into a larger pot as the roots will grow through it much faster and very quickly grow a large plant.

From about the beginning of April the greenhouse should be shaded. It is important to remember that tuberous begonias thrive when grown in cool but not cold – never below 50°F (10°C) – well ventilated conditions. When the plants are moved to the unheated greenhouse, ensure vents and doors are left open when conditions allow. The movement of air is essential for growing good quality plants.

And so it goes on, potting up and more potting up – the life of a begonia grower is a pretty repetitious one but the final results will be well worth all the extra effort. Now is the time to decide whether to grow the tubers for cut blooms or for pot plants or maybe some of both. (For growing for cut blooms *see* Chapter 4; for growing pot plants *see* Chapter 5.) Also, now is the time if you want more cuttings to remove unwanted side shoots (*see* Chapter 11).

Whether the begonias have been grown for cut blooms or for pot plants at some stage the plants will have been stopped, that is, the growing tips will have been removed to produce larger flowers, so that by

The plant has been removed from its pot so the compost can dry out more quickly.

the middle of September the plants will have finished flowering. The plants now know that it is time to prepare for dormancy. This is the period when the begonias rest, recover and replace the energy that they have used producing the beautiful flowers that have been enjoyed during the summer.

As they start to go into dormancy, all the goodness and moisture from the stem and leaves starts to go back into the tubers, making them swell. The plants may start to throw up shoots from around the base of the stems but it is really too late in the season to start rooting cuttings again, so they are left to their own devices and soon die back. To help them go into dormancy the adult plants should be given a half teaspoon of potash sprinkled around the top of the pots and watered in. This is to harden the tubers off. Watch out for any stem rot which must be cut out and treated or the tuber could be lost (*see* Chapter 12).

At the end of September or beginning of October all watering of the adult plants should be stopped. Continuing to water will make it difficult to dry the compost in the pots when the plants go into dormancy and may possibly lead to rotting of the tubers. The plants themselves are beginning look dilapidated. The bottom leaves start to go yellow and drop off and the stems start to drop off in segments. Cutting the stems back by about a third will speed up the process, but patience is needed to allow nature to take its course without forcing.

As a precaution the whole greenhouse should be sprayed with a fungicide to try and delay the inevitable mildew. At this time of year mildew is not a great problem but the longer it can be delayed the better. All the plants are probably squashed together to fit them all in the greenhouse, and all the vents and the door are regularly being closed to try and keep the greenhouse warmer especially when frost is forecast. All this will encourage mildew. This is the exact opposite of the free air circulation that has been advocated all year. Fallen leaves and debris should be picked up as soon as possible. Keeping the greenhouse clean will help to prevent botrytis.

When the stems start to fall off, the tubers can be harvested. It is very tempting to 'help' them to fall off, but try to resist the temptation and let them fall off naturally. This will help later when it is time to remove the callus from the tuber.

Watch out for pots that do not look as if they are drying out. It may be that there is a poor root system that is not drawing up the moisture. Remove the plant from the pot, inverting the pot, and stand the plant on the upturned pot. This will enable the air circulation to dry the compost more quickly.

This is the time of the year to watch the weather forecasts. If there are frost warnings, switch on the heating to keep the greenhouse free of frost. If there is no heating, use newspapers or Agrifleece to cover

The same tuber with the callus flicked up ready for removal.

This tuber has been dried and cleaned off; the callus is still intact.

The callus now removed, the tubers are dusted with sulphur powder and are ready to be put away for the winter period.

The tubers are left on the slatted shelving to dry out completely before being stored for the winter. Note the cuttings are still in growth.

the plants. A dry atmosphere at this juncture is arguably even more important than warmth.

When the plant stems eventually drop off, remove the tuber from the pot and carefully remove some of the compost. Do not remove all the compost or the skin of the tuber may be damaged. By allowing the air to dry the compost for a few more days, this gives the soft skin time to harden. Finally take a soft brush and clean the tuber.

Now the tuber is left to dry and the skin of the tuber to harden. This process takes a couple of weeks or so. The final job to do before the tuber is put away for the winter is to remove the callus from the tuber. This can be one of the trickiest parts of begonia growing. It is important to remove the callus on adult tubers or they can rot during storage. The callus is found where the stem joined the tuber. Judge when the tuber is dry and using a strong thumbnail or a blunt knife try to prise off the callus.

This can be quite a surprise when done correctly for the first time. If the callus has come off cleanly, the top of the tuber will look just like a crater on the surface of the moon. If the callus does not come off cleanly, or the tuber feels soft or spongy, leave it to dry for a few more days and try again. If there is still doubt that the callus has not been removed take a sharp knife and cut away any residual stem from the tuber. When the callus has been removed, either prised off or cut off, the exposed wound should be dusted with sulphur.

The tubers are now ready to be put away for the winter. They can be stored in open trays, or wrapped in newspaper, or buried in dry peat. They should be stored in a cool dry place but they must be kept frost free. The tubers should be inspected regularly to see if there is any rotting, which should be dealt with. We now look forward to next year when we can start all over again.

Having had the bleach treatment, these adult tubers are drying off prior to storing away for the winter.

CHAPTER 4

Growing cut blooms

A cut bloom is just the male central bloom together with a small portion of stem detached from the begonia plant. The blooms are placed in cups and displayed on specially constructed boards, either single bloom, three blooms, six blooms or even twelve blooms at the major shows.

Growing cut blooms means growing just one bloom per plant, a procedure that is primarily undertaken for exhibiting at flower shows. The main advantages of exhibiting cut blooms, compared to pot plants, are that cut blooms are far easier to transport to the shows and that they do not have to be collected when the show is over; also the plants take less room in the greenhouse. The main disadvantages of exhibiting cut blooms, compared to pot plants, are that the blooms need to be timed to be at their pristine best on the show day and also that after the blooms have been cut for the show there is no further colour in the greenhouse.

The first thing to consider when growing for

This is what we are aiming for.

exhibition is the tubers, what varieties to grow and where to get them. With regard to the varieties, there is a wide range of blooms to be seen around the shows and in other people's greenhouses. Unfortunately it is not possible to grow them all. It is a good idea to talk to some of the exhibitors and to ask their opinion on what varieties should be grown as a start. Some begonias are easier to grow than others; some keep better than others; and some begonias have different growing habits. So it does make sense to take the advice of people who have been growing for a number of years.

As for where to source the named varieties of begonias, there are two choices. There are a few commercial nurseries in the UK which supply the large double tuberous begonias (*see* page 107). The benefit of buying from a commercial nursery is that they will offer a wide range of varieties and if there are any problems they will probably listen to you with a sympathetic ear. Begonia tubers are expensive because hybridizing new varieties takes a lot of time and effort. Propagation is not easy and commercial nurseries have overheads and wages to pay. The other source for named tuberous begonia varieties is from fellow growers who may be willing and kind enough to part with one or two plants or sell a couple of tubers at the back end of the year. Joining one of the Begonia Societies is the best way of meeting fellow growers (*see* page 108).

To grow any sort of a decent bloom, two- or three-year-old tubers are best. These tubers should be free of holes (suspect vine weevil damage if holes are present), and appear nice and plump. Do not expect them to be round; begonia tubers come in all shapes and sizes.

Listed below are ten varieties of tuberous begonias that will be suitable when starting to grow cut blooms for exhibition. These varieties are easy to grow, easily obtainable, give a superb colour range and the prices should be reasonable.

- 'Mrs Elizabeth McLauchlan' – very easy to grow, a lovely pink bicolour and propagates well.
- 'Linda Jackson' – a large red, rather tall grower, easily recognized by its leaves, it throws plenty of cuttings.

- 'Monica Bryce' – the best all-round yellow available.
- 'Tahiti' – a great orange, easy to grow, rather tall, reliable.
- 'Falstaff' – very strong growing, short in habit, deep rose pink, worth including in any collection.
- 'Bernat Klein' – has been around a long time, a tall grower with beautiful white blooms and thick petals.
- 'Cancan' – a very eye-catching yellow picotee with a red edge, very easy to grow and propagate, a tall grower.
- 'Roy Hartley' – one of the great begonias of all time, salmon pink.
- 'Ruby Young' – a much sought-after cream picotee, a modern variety that everyone ought to have in their collection.
- 'Sweet Dreams' – a beautiful pink with layers of wavy petals; most exhibitors have grown this at one time or another.

The compost used for growing exhibition blooms is no different from that for growing begonias for pleasure, nor is the starting into growth procedure. A good time to plant them into the hotbox or propagator would be around the second or third week in March. The starting up and potting on procedure for adult tubers is described in Chapter 3.

When the begonia plants are in 4in or 5in (1 litre) pots and growing away nicely, all the side shoots need to be removed as soon as it is possible. Obviously if the side shoots are required for cuttings they can only be removed when they are big enough. However, if they are not needed they should be rubbed off as soon as they start to form. The greenhouse should be shaded no later than the beginning of April to prevent burned or scorched plants. On dull days a foliar feed should be given, preferably early in the morning. The intention is to build a thick stemmed, strong plant. Feeding into the pots is not done at this stage, as the plants are not yet into their final pots. Keep checking the root system. If the roots are beginning to show the plant should be potted on again. By this time some of the nutrients will have been washed out through watering and the growing plant itself will have used up a fair bit of nutrient. By potting on and adding more compost containing fertilizers, the plant is fed. Foliar feeding should continue when the days are dull and all flower buds should be removed as soon as they appear.

The root systems have been checked once again and the plants are now ready to go in to their final pots, usually 3 or 4 litre (7 or 8in) pots. Once they are in their final pots a cane needs to be placed behind each plant to support the stem. A begonia will normally produce a flower pointing the same way the leaves are pointing, so the cane is inserted in the side of the pot away from the pointing leaves. Because the plant is eventually going to have to support a large flower growing at its tip, the cane is placed so that it leans slightly backwards. Stout bamboo canes can be used or better still the plastic coated steel canes which are much easier to clean and will last for ever. Push the cane down to the bottom of the pot, firming the compost around it, and tie the plant stem to the cane. At first one tie will be sufficient but as the plant grows, further ties will be necessary. The tie used is quite important: it should be a polypropylene tie that water runs off, preferably one that is wide so that it does not cut into the stem. If a string or twine tie is used, it can get wet and cause the stem to rot.

Soon after the plants are in their final pots they can be fed with a high nitrogen feed such as Chempak No 2 at half the recommended strength. The plants will be growing strongly at this time. When the plants have had a couple of feeds of the half strength Chempak No 2, the leaves will take on a darker colour and the stem will start getting thicker. It is getting closer to the time for selecting the buds that will be allowed to flower. Now is the time to harden the root system. This can be done by feeding with a fertilizer with an N.P.K. of say 15-30-15, the emphasis being on the phosphate (it is phosphate that encourages the roots to grow).

About nine weeks before the show date stop removing the flower buds. The flower buds are now allowed to develop, so there will be a choice to pick from when it is time to select the chosen bud for the exhibition bloom.

It is about this time that some thought must be given as to when the blooms have to flower. There is one date that is definite: the date of the show. The other dates in the growing calendar are not fixed.

They are at best estimates gathered from years of experience. Stopping dates are defined as the number of days it will take a bloom of a particular variety to be open at its best from a bud 1⅛in or 30mm in diameter (the size of an old ten-pence piece). Different varieties take different numbers of days to open from a bud this size. It is worthwhile trying to find out stopping dates for particular varieties from other local growers.

The stopping dates quoted below will give a good starting guide. The most important thing is to keep a record of actual stopping dates found and also note the weather conditions, and then timings can be adjusted for the following year. This is the way to improve your results. Unfortunately there is no

STOPPING DATES

A stopping date is the time between having a bud of 1⅛in or 30mm diameter, and the bloom being fully open and at its best. It must be remembered that all the dates given here are not written in stone. They are estimates given after years of growing in the East Lancashire area.

Some examples of stopping dates:

'Anne Crawford'	42 days
'Apricot Delight'	38–42 days
'Avalanche'	42 days
'Bali Hi'	35 days
'Beryl Rhodes'	40–42 days
'Cancan'	38–42 days
'Coppelia'	40 days
'Falstaff'	42 days
'Full Moon'	40–42 days
'Geoff Bizley'	42 days
'Isobelle Keenan'	38–40 days
'Kathryn Hartley'	42 days
'Linda Jackson'	42 days
'Mrs E. McLauchlan'	38–40 days
'Powder Puff'	38–40 days
'Ruby Young'	38–40 days
'Snowgoose'	42 days
'Tahiti'	40–42 days
'Tom Brownlee'	42+ days
'Whispers'	38–42 days

way of controlling the weather. If there is a scorching heat wave some of the blooms will come early. If the weather is dull and cool some of the blooms will be late. However, there is the consolation that the other competitors will be having the same problems.

For example, I give the variety 'Bernat Klein' thirty-five days to open and be at its best from a bud 1⅛in or 30mm in diameter. So I would count back thirty-five days from the date of the flower show and then look at my 'Bernat Klein' plants and try and find a bud of this size. Because I grow three or four plants of this variety, I would probably find one or two. I would then try to find one slightly smaller than 1⅛in or 30mm and possibly one slightly larger. By selecting one smaller and one larger I am trying to hedge my bets so that I should get one or two blooms spot on for the show date. Having selected my buds, the individual plants are stopped. That means the growing tips are pinched out. All the other buds are removed, just leaving the one selected bud per plant.

It is now forty-nine days to the show. Of the recommended varieties, 'Roy Hartley' has the longest stopping date of forty-nine days and so it is the first plant to work on to select the buds that will be flowered. The pots are carefully lifted on to a table and given a good inspection. Now is the time to add another tie if it is required. The top leaves are carefully parted and the buds examined. It may be apparent straight away that the first bud is too large, so look at the next one. Is that one nearer the correct size? A bud stick is very handy; this is simply a piece of stiff white card cut out to the exact size of an old ten pence piece (1⅛in or 30mm diameter), and glued into the end of a kebab stick. The bud stick can be held against a bud to determine its size without fingers getting in the way and perhaps causing damage to the bud. When the correct sized bud has been chosen, all the other buds, except our chosen bud, are removed and the growing tip of the plant is pinched out. Now all the energy of the plant will go up the stem and into the flower bud. The plant has only one thing it wants to do and that is to reproduce, and that means the flower is going to get all the energy. Now the task of taking the buds is repeated on the other plants as the stopping days arrive.

When all the buds have been secured, it is good practice to turn any picotee varieties so that the bloom is facing the glass at the sides of the greenhouse. This improves the colour and makes the picotee edge of the bloom more even. One exception to this is the variety 'Ruby Young' which should be grown in a low position near to the door of the greenhouse.

Until now the concentration has been on growing a strong plant, but now the concentration is on the flower. From now on the fertilizer is switched from a high phosphate feed to a high potash feed to feed the flower. I use Chempak No 4 at a diluted rate of a quarter of the recommended strength, to be fed into the pot at every other watering. This can be increased to half strength if thought necessary, but care must be taken: too much feed can cause colour run and increase the risk of double centres.

When the diameter of the bud gets to about 2½in (6.5cm), it is time to put polystyrene plates behind the bud. This is done to protect the bud from any damage. Polystyrene plates can be purchased from most supermarkets. These should be 9in (23cm) diameter. The centre of the plate is marked and a ½in (12mm) hole made in the centre of the plate. With a craft knife two parallel cuts are made from the centre hole to the edge of the plate giving a ½in (12mm) slot. The plate is very carefully slid down

A 9" POLYSTYRENE DINNER PLATE.
½"-¾" Hole in the centre
Cut through to edge of plate.

The polystyrene plate.

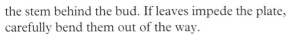
The two side-buds are removed.

Supporting the bloom using a bloom support.

the stem behind the bud. If leaves impede the plate, carefully bend them out of the way.

At the same time the two small flower buds that are growing at the back of the chosen bud are removed. These two buds may be male or female, and should be removed carefully with a thin pair of scissors.

As the bloom grows it will start to hang down with its own weight, so it needs to be supported. Commercially made supports are available for begonias. These supports are made from two pieces of thin stiff wire with a sliding adjustment at the centre. At the top they are formed into a 'U' shape about ¾in (2cm) wide and ¾in (2cm) deep. When the flower needs support, the plant support is carefully pushed into the plant pot, beneath the flower but avoiding the tuber. Very carefully the flower stem is lifted until the stem behind the neck of the flower rests in the U shape. Finally the height of the support is adjusted until it just takes the weight of the flower. As an added precaution, to prevent any chafing to

the stem of the bloom, a small layer of Dacron is placed in the bottom of the U. Practise first on a bloom that is not going to the show.

The alternative to using commercial bloom supports is to tie the blooms back to the support cane. The plant cane will need to be taller than the plant and to prevent the tie cutting into the stem some sort of synthetic tape about ½in (12mm) wide is required. A medium-sized rubber band is wrapped two or three times around the top of the cane, and slid down the cane until it is 3–4in (7.5–10cm) higher than the top of the bloom. This rubber band is to stop the tape from sliding down the cane once it has been tied in position. The tape is carefully slipped between the back of the polystyrene plate and the plant stem, and gently slid up the stem until the weight of the bloom is supported at the neck. The two ends of the tape are wrapped round the support cane above the rubber band and tied off. These ties will have to be adjusted occasionally.

As the flowers get larger, the back petals of the

Supporting the bloom by tying back.

blooms will come into more contact with the polystyrene plates. On really hot days, the back petals can actually stick to the plate. A small wad of Dacron between the back petals and the plate will solve the problem. Dacron can also be used to help improve flower petals that are slightly twisted or bent, by tucking a small wad of Dacron carefully underneath the offending petal. Within a few days the kink or slight bend should have improved. (Dacron is a trade name for a synthetic filling material used in the production of soft furnishings. The beauty of Dacron is the spring in it. It compresses very tightly between the fingertips, and on release it expands nicely to its normal bulk again.)

Apart from the blooms, now is the time to consider what else is necessary when staging an exhibit. A lot of care has been taken growing the blooms and care also needs to be taken getting them to the show bench. Large cardboard boxes are required to transport the blooms. Spare bloom boxes from a florist are ideal. Orchid or bloom tubes

can also be purchased from the florist. These will be used as miniature vases for the bloom stems whilst being transported. A large bag of Dacron can be purchased from an upholsterer. This will be used to pack round the blooms to prevent damage whilst being transported. (Dacron is similar in appearance to cotton wool but is preferred to cotton wool because it does not hold water and also it works out cheaper.) Bloom boards for displaying the blooms are usually supplied by the show organizers. However, it is up to the exhibitor to supply the polystyrene drinking cups which will hold the blooms on the boards. It is worthwhile purchasing cups of varying sizes because the holes in the bloom boards can differ slightly. Lemonade (not the diet variety) is used as staging fluid to put in the cups to keep the blooms fresh during the show. Before the show day, if there are any sub-standard blooms or blooms that have peaked too early, it would be prudent to practise cutting and picking a bloom up, inserting the stem into a bloom tube, and packing the cut bloom into Dacron in the cardboard bloom box.

When you decide to compete at a show, you will receive a schedule, which will include an application form. The schedule is a list of classes together with a list of rules for the show. When you read the rules on the show schedule, you will find something like this: 'Benching for exhibitors 6am till 9am. Exhibitors to remove all rubbish and leave the hall by 9am.' (Benching is the term used for setting up the blooms at the show venue). So you have to be at the show ground just before 6am, and you need to work out how long it will take you to drive from home to the show venue, taking your time. Working backwards, decide what time the blooms have to be cut and packed into their boxes. These things must be worked out beforehand. Always leave yourself plenty of time to cut and pack your blooms. Some mistakes can be costly on the show bench. However, leave the cutting of your blooms as late as you possibly can. The less time they spend in the bloom tubes the better. Make yourself a list of things to do and things to take with you, so that you will not get to the show and realize that you have forgotten something.

The day of the show arrives. Before setting off for the show there is a lot to do. If it is in the middle of the night, make sure there is plenty of light to see by,

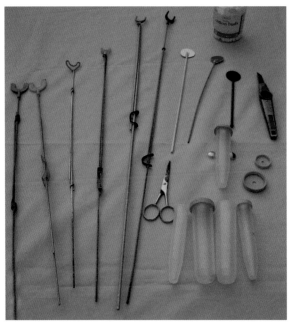

A few essential pieces of equipment: (left) a selection of different sorts of bloom supports; (bottom right) different sizes of bloom tubes with rubber tops; (top right) three different sorts of bud sticks (the black one is a cocktail stirrer); (far right) a craft knife, handy because the blade can be retracted inside the handle; (centre) sharp pointed scissors; (top right) cotton wool buds for removing any dross from blooms.

right hand cut the flower stem as far down as possible, and lift the bloom away. At this point you can either carefully slide your polystyrene plate off your bloom, or you can leave your bloom sitting on the plate until you get to the show. I prefer to remove it when cutting my bloom. With your right hand pick up a sharp craft knife and cut the end of the bloom stem at a steep angle. Put the knife down and pick up a bloom tube and push the sharpened edge of the bloom stem into the tube. This may need quite a bit of pressure depending on the thickness of the flower stem. As the stem goes into the tube, the water will be seen to rise up around the flower stem. This is how the flower will stay fresh until it gets to the show.

Now the bloom must be placed into the box. By carefully turning your left hand so the bloom faces upwards, and with your right hand, palm upwards, spread your fingers wide and take the weight of the bloom. Release your left hand from the flower stem, and palm upwards, spread your fingers wide and place underneath the bloom so that now you have both hands supporting the bloom. Gently place the bloom into the box and lay it on to the nest of Dacron that was made previously. The Dacron is soft and spongy, so there will be no trouble pushing your hands, one at a time, into the Dacron and slowly removing them. All that is left to do now is to fluff the Dacron up a little. Take a piece of the masking tape and place it over the end of the bloom tube and stick it to the bottom of the box. This will hold it in place until it gets to the show. Now add some more Dacron and make another nest for the next bloom. Again, it is strongly recommended that these procedures be rehearsed beforehand. Keep practising holding the bloom in your left hand, inserting the stem into the bloom tube, and finally learning to support the bloom on your upturned palms.

On arrival at the show ground, look for the show steward and ask for your exhibitor's pack. This will contain the show cards and numbers and your classes. Walk along the tables and find out where your classes are and check that the show boards are correct. Next, try to find a table so that you can work at a comfortable height. Fetch your bloom box or boxes, along with your box of bits and pieces, containing cups, knife, scissors, damp cloth and dry hand towel. Firstly, wipe the exhibition boards with

whether in the greenhouse, garage or kitchen. First the bloom boxes have to be prepared. Put the bloom box on the bench and place a big wad of Dacron in it, making a nest at one end, where the first bloom will go. The bloom tubes are then half filled with fresh water, the rubber tops replaced and the tubes placed in 6in (15cm) half pots. A few strips of masking tape, about 6in (15cm) long, will be required later to secure the bloom tubes to the bottom of the bloom box.

The only thing not yet done is to cut a bloom, as mentioned earlier. If this has been practised it should not be too much of a problem. Pick one of the plants that will be going to the show and carefully turn it so it is facing either to the left or to the right. If you are right-handed, grip the bloom with the finger and thumb of your left hand, as close to the neck of the bloom as possible, and with your

CONSTRUCTING BLOOM BOARDS

Plans are shown for the simple construction of a twelve-bloom board, a six-bloom board, a three-bloom board and a single bloom board. These boards are flat faced (sometimes twelve-boards are faced in three steps).

In all instances, the sides and ends are fastened together using Conti blocks, two at the wide ends and one at the narrow ends. Conti blocks have been used for ease of assembly and for dismantling after use, so the boards may be stored flat. The top may also be held in place using Conti blocks if desired. Alternatively the tops may be held in place by gluing 3in (7.5cm) strips of ½in (12mm) Velcro tape to the corner and centre of each side and the corresponding undersides of the tops. Six Conti blocks are required to assemble each board. If using them to fasten the top on, extra blocks will be required.

The cup hole centres are 9in (23cm) apart. Cup hole diameters are dependent on the size of the polystyrene cups used; usually they are about 2½in (6.5cm) in diameter.

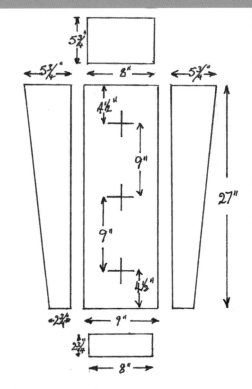

Plan for a three-board.
Cutting list
Top: one piece of plywood, 27in × 9in × ¼in (69cm × 23cm × 6mm)
Sides: two pieces of plywood, 27in × 5¾in × ½in (69cm × 15cm × 12mm) to be cut on a taper
End: one piece of plywood, 8in × 5¾in × ½in (20cm × 15cm × 12mm)
End: one piece of plywood, 8in × 2¾in × ½in (20cm × 7cm × 12mm)

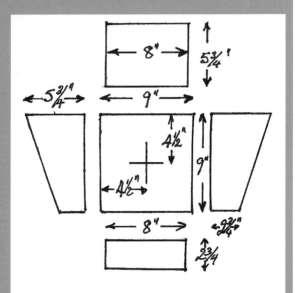

Plan for a single-board.
Cutting list
Top: one piece of plywood, 9in × 9in × ¼in (23cm × 23cm × 6mm)
Sides: two pieces of plywood, 9in × 5¾in × ½in (23cm × 15cm × 12mm) to be cut on a taper
End: one piece of plywood, 8in × 5¾in × ½in (20cm × 15cm × 12mm)
End: one piece of plywood, 8in × 2¾in × ½in (20cm × 7cm × 12mm)

When finished the boxes are traditionally finished in black paint.

Usually exhibitors' bloom boards are supplied by the society arranging the show. However, at some of the smaller shows you may be required to supply your own.

To the novice cut bloom grower they are useful to have at home for practising the handling of blooms and positioning them in their cups. Practice makes perfect and it is better to practise on spare or damaged blooms at home rather than good ones at the show.

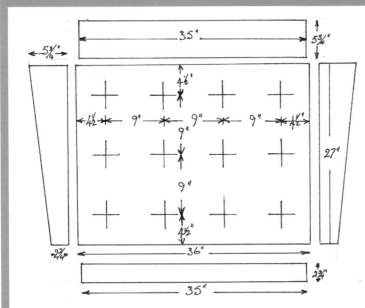

Plan for a twelve-board.

Cutting list

Top: one piece of plywood, 36in×27in×⅜in (91cm×69cm×1cm)

Sides: two pieces of plywood, 27in×5¾in×½in (69cm×15cm×12mm) to be cut on a taper

End: one piece of plywood, 35in×5¾in×½in (89cm×15cm×12mm)

End: one piece of plywood, 35in×2¾in×½in (89cm×7cm×12mm)

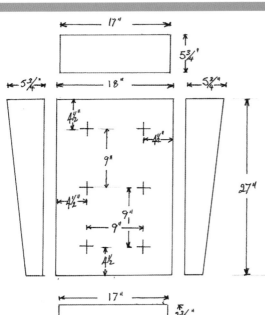

Plan for a six-board.

Cutting list

Top: one piece of plywood, 27in×18in×¼in (69cm×46cm×6mm)

Sides: two pieces of plywood, 27in×5¾in×½in (69cm×15cm×12mm) to be cut on a taper

End: one piece of plywood, 17in×5¾in×½in (43cm×1cm×12mm)

End: one piece of plywood, 17in×2¾in×½in (43cm×7cm×12mm)

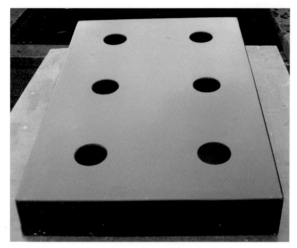

A typical show board for six cut blooms.

a damp cloth. The chances are that they have not been used since last year and they may be grubby or dusty. These boards are for your blooms so be proud of them. Take the polystyrene or plastic cups and place them firmly into the holes. Try two cups in each to start with, and fill with lemonade to about an inch from the top of the cup.

The next step is to place the blooms into their respective cups. If you are showing a three-board, the bloom at the back is the first bloom to be placed, and then work downwards. This is so you are not leaning over the blooms. You should have already considered what varieties and colours you want, and where you want them. The bloom that is to be placed at the back is carefully removed from the bloom box, preferably with both hands palm upwards, fingers outstretched. Now hold the bloom

Side view with polystyrene cups inserted (one at the front, three at the back), but the numbers of cups can vary depending on the size and depth of the bloom.

in your left hand, as you did when you cut your bloom from the plant, and remove the bloom tube. The last job is to estimate the length of the flower stem required in relation to the cup it is being placed in. Generally 2½in (6.5cm) will be fine. Supporting the bloom with both hands, lower the bloom into its cup. The stem of the bloom is in the front, so lower it from the back of the cup towards the front. Ensure the bloom is sitting nicely on the cup, then release it. Repeat the process until your entry is complete. Fill in your variety cards and entry form. The job is now finished.

One final note: it is always worthwhile to take along two or three spare blooms. Sometimes you will find a bloom may be damaged or will have been dropped. If you have a spare you can change it. When you are happy with your exhibit clean up your rubbish and leave the show area.

Now it is up to the judges. Judges are only human: when they look at blooms they know they will not find perfection. However, they will expect to see clean blooms. Try not to exhibit blooms that are past their best. It is preferable to show a young bloom. Travel damage is different from damage caused by bad handling. The former might be forgiven, but the latter is frowned upon. The person who never made a mistake never grew anything, and one certain thing is that you will rarely make the same mistake twice. When you enter a show of any sort it is always nice to get a card, particularly a red one. If you don't, do not give up; try harder next year. I would like to wish any would-be exhibitor the very best of luck when he or she decides to have a try at exhibiting these wonderful flowers.

CHAMPIONSHIP GROWERS

We have looked at growing for exhibition. Now we will take it a step further and have a look at how the championship growers set their stalls out. The ultimate prizes for cut bloom begonia growing in the UK are the twelve-board championship classes at the main begonia shows at Ayr and Birmingham. This means twelve cut blooms of no fewer than nine varieties. The growers who enter championship competitions will be altogether more dedicated, even probably just growing for this one class in one show. They have probably been exhibiting for

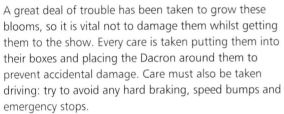

A great deal of trouble has been taken to grow these blooms, so it is vital not to damage them whilst getting them to the show. Every care is taken putting them into their boxes and placing the Dacron around them to prevent accidental damage. Care must also be taken driving: try to avoid any hard braking, speed bumps and emergency stops.

several years and know their begonia varieties, and how to grow them, inside out.

So let us take a look at how the champion growers do things. Firstly, the varieties of blooms to be grown are selected very carefully. To win a twelve-board championship class, not only are large blooms needed, but also blooms of exceptional quality and form, and the blooms have to be at their very best on the show day. The championship grower has room in his greenhouses only for growing top quality blooms, so he has to be absolutely ruthless in the selection of varieties that are to be grown and merit a place on his twelve-board. An old grower once said, 'Eh lad, a poor bloom takes up the same space in a greenhouse as a good one, why waste time on a poor 'un?' Of course he was right and on more than one occasion I have had reason to think on his words. The different varieties in the different colours will be studied and the best two or three varieties in each colour will be selected. For example, two reds ('Tom Brownlee' and 'Goliath'), two yellows ('Monica Bryce' and 'Ann Crawford'), two whites ('Avalanche' and 'Bernat Klein'), and so the list goes on through the colours. Now to the hard part: the varieties he has not selected have to be discarded from the collection. The chosen varieties are now grown in multiples, such as six Tom Brownlees, six Goliaths, six Monica Bryces six Ann Crawfords and so on. The greenhouse now, instead of having fifty different varieties will now have say eighteen different varieties in whatever multiples the space permits. The varieties chosen will almost certainly be varieties that grow to a good size, that will have good shape and form and probably, but not neces-sarily, have a rose-bud centre. They should not be prone to colour run, nor plagued by double centres. Some varieties are known to hang around for a couple of days when grown to their optimum size before going over prematurely and wilting. All of these points will have been taken into consideration. These chosen varieties are known as bankers.

By growing fewer varieties, but in multiples, more cuttings of these varieties will be available to main-tain and replace stock when necessary. Growing in this manner will mean that when it comes to selecting buds for the show there will be more buds to select from and stopping dates can be staggered so that on the show date if one bloom is just going over, another bloom may well be coming to its very best. Growing blooms like this gives more chance of producing a very good exhibition twelve-board, and as more growers are starting to grow this way it gives the judges more of a headache when selecting a winning board.

STAGING A TWELVE-BOARD

In an ideal world, an exhibitor would take twelve identically sized blooms, all in pristine condition and stage a perfect board. In reality an exhibitor will probably be struggling to pick twelve blooms good enough to place on a twelve-board, so staging them effectively is important to maximize the chance of a winning board.

When I staged my first twelve-board I was lucky enough to be advised by one of the best cut bloom exhibitors in the country and I have followed his advice ever since:

- Clean and dry the staging board, put the cups in place, and put the staging solution (lemonade) in the cups.
- Make sure that your hands are clean and dry, as dirty and sweaty hands will mark the blooms.
- Twelve-boards are always displayed as three rows of four blooms. Place the largest blooms at the back of the board because any gaps between blooms will always look worse on the back row.
- The judges' eyes will almost always be drawn to the four corner blooms on the board, so the corner blooms need to be bright and eye catching. Reds, whites, yellows, oranges or perhaps a gaudy picotee, rather than a pastel shade, should be used as the corner blooms.
- Take a look at the blooms that you have to select from and then decide on the two blooms to go on the top left and top right corners of the board.
- There is always a minimum number of varieties allowed on a twelve-board. Be sure to have at least the number of varieties specified in the schedule. If you have to use two or more blooms of the same variety on the board, space them as far away from each other as possible. No matter how good the blooms are, there are bound to be differences in size or quality, so it

makes good sense to place them away from each other so that the differences are not as apparent.

- Now place the top two corner blooms very carefully into their cups. I also keep to one side the two blooms that I have chosen for the bottom corners. Then it is a matter of choosing two blooms for the middle of the top row that contrast in colour with the two top corner blooms.
- Once the top four blooms are in their cups it is time to have a look from the end of the table to make sure that the blooms are at about the same height; it may be that one or two of them will need an extra cup or two to make them all level.
- Once the top row is completed, move on to the centre row, starting at the left-hand side. Being conscious of the colours selected for the bottom corners, try to choose a bloom with a colour that blends nicely with the top and bottom corner blooms, and carefully place the bloom in the cup. Moving over to the right-hand side of the middle row, select another bloom and place it in that cup.
- Now the two blooms that were chosen for the bottom two are placed in their cups. The top row and the two sides are now complete. Step back to see how things look, whether the blooms are balanced, whether there any colour clashes. If all is well there are just the four centre and bottom blooms to put in place.
- There will now be fewer blooms to select from, so if there were any blooms slightly smaller than the others I would recommend using these on the bottom row. If the board has been made up of hard solid colours, a good white picotee bloom would lighten the board up.
- The two middle row centre blooms are placed in their cups and checked from the side to make sure they are level.

- Finally the two bottom row centre blooms are placed in their cups and checked to make sure they are level.
- Now stand back and check the board over to ensure that you are happy with your choice of blooms and that the blooms will be looking at the judge when he or she is standing in front of them. The heights are once again checked. (If I have used blooms with camellia shaped centres I make sure that the centres are facing the same way, either facing across the board or up and down it.)
- The spare blooms are placed under the staging table.
- Half an hour before judging, check your board for the last time. If one of the blooms is weak or drooping, you still have time to change it. Every time a bloom is handled there is more chance of damaging it. This is especially so if it is a red bloom. It is handy to have a spare box that has a couple of holes cut into it to hold a couple of cups. These can be used to hold blooms until they are ready to be used, or to change a bloom over. It is a simple job to lift a bloom and place it into the spare cup whilst reselecting another bloom, thus causing minimal damage.
- Now it is time to leave the tent or hall and await the decision of the judges. Exhibitors are not allowed to remain in the area while judging is in progress and the public is also excluded.

Note: make sure that the correct number of cultivars has been adhered to, as specified in the schedule. If using an un-named hybrid, this can be labelled as a seedling but make sure it is significantly different from any of the other varieties on the board so there is no dispute over the number of separate varieties on the board.

CHAPTER 5

Growing pot plants

This is what we are aiming for.

If you are not growing a begonia for cut blooms, then you are growing a pot plant. Pot plants for showing come in several different classes and whether the aim is to grow pot plants for showing or whether growing purely for pleasure, it is as well to look at the options.

Typical classes at a major begonia show are:

- A multi-stemmed plant with side shoots. This is a plant with several basal shoots each carrying side shoots.
- A single-stemmed plant with either two or three side shoots.
- A single-stemmed plant with no side shoots – commonly shown in Scotland.

Most named varieties will produce a decent pot plant because bloom size is not as important as when growing for cut blooms. A consideration for a pot plant class will be the growth habit, preferably tall and long jointed (a cut bloom variety may often have a more squat form).

Here is a short list of varieties that will give good results when grown as pot plants:

- 'Avalanche' – a very good white with wavy petals.
- 'Apricot Delight' – a beautiful colour, good branching habit, well formed blooms with plenty of layers of petals.

A good example of how single-stemmed pot plants are shown in Scotland. If space in the greenhouse is at a premium, growing single-stemmed plants can save a lot of room, enabling more plants to be grown.

- 'Coppelia' – a white picotee with a red edge, very clean and sharp looking, large blooms with plenty of petals, an eye catcher.
- 'Dr Eric Catterall' – a very good red, branching habit, large flowers with plenty of petals.
- 'Fairylight' – an old variety, very attractive white picotee.
- 'George McCormick' – a beautiful eye-catching white picotee with a red edge.
- 'Jessie Cruikshank' – an older variety but one of the best, a white picotee.
- 'Kathryn Hartley' – a sport of Roy Hartley, pale pink with large, well-formed flowers.
- 'Lancelot' – one of the more recent whites with a pleasing form and nice centre.
- 'Linda Jackson' – a very good red, a tall grower with superbly shaped blooms.
- 'Monica Bryce' – an excellent yellow with plenty of basal and side shoots and well-shaped blooms.
- 'Moonlight' – a creamy-white bloom with a rosebud centre.
- 'Mrs E. McLauchlan' – a beautiful bicolour, good for every reason: blooms, habit, form, and propagates easily.
- 'Powder Puff' – a very pale pink, tall grower with well formed large blooms.
- 'Roy Hartley' – a great old variety, salmon pink with magnificent blooms.
- 'Ruby Young' – a superb cream picotee with wonderful blooms, an eye catcher.
- 'Sweet Dreams' – a gorgeous pink with wavy petals.
- 'Tahiti' – a nice orange, tall grower with large, well-formed blooms; grow in good light to prevent a white centre.
- 'Whispers' – a modern variety, creamy-white, a tall grower.
- 'Ziggy' – a marvellous white picotee with perfect blooms and form.

For the purpose of this chapter we will be looking at growing a multi-stemmed plant which has, say, four basal stems, with at least two side shoots on each stem, with each basal stem and each side shoot carrying two flowers, so the plant will have the potential to carry twenty-four blooms or more.

Some of the techniques described will also be useful for growing the other classes of pot plants. It is very worthwhile writing notes and comments for each plant grown, such as dates on which adjustments were made, stopping dates, feeding schedules and final results. Then the following year adjustments can be made to get even better results. Serious exhibitors will grow two or three pots for each show class that is entered. By doing this, the timing dates can be staggered giving a better chance of getting a plant with blooms just right on the day of the show.

The growing of a multi-stemmed pot plant is, to begin with, not so different from growing a single-stemmed plant, with one main exception: older, large tubers are needed to give the required number of basal stems. Large tubers are selected that have several callus scars on top and these are started off in the normal way in the hot bed or propagator. Pot plants really need to be started off around the middle of February. Starting them a month before the cut bloom tubers gives them that extra time to develop into a good sized plant. Tubers are planted in trays in a propagator or directly into a hot bed in 50:50 multi-purpose compost and perlite as described in Chapter 3. While they are in the hot bed or propagator a number of shoots should start off on the tuber. Hopefully there will be four strong ones. Ideally, three of the shoots will have their leaves pointing outwards at approximately 120° to each other. The flowers will normally face the same way the leaves are pointing so that with these three shoots the plant in bloom will give an all-round viewing angle. The fourth shoot is selected to give flowers in the centre of the plant. If there are other unwanted or weaker spindly shoots they should be rubbed off so that all growth is concentrated on the selected shoots.

When the shoots are about 2in (5cm) high and are growing well, the root ball should be checked and when necessary potted up in to a correctly sized pot. The plants should not be allowed to check. Either the pots should be put back in the hot bed, or the greenhouse should be heated. For this first potting I use a peat-based compost, but for subsequent potting I use John Innes No 2 compost. The plants are now grown on, being potted up as required, until they are in their final pots. The final pot size is typically a 5 litre (9in) pot but sometimes this may be specified by the show schedule.

When the plants are in their final pots and the basal shoots are about 9in (23cm) or so above the rim of the pot, the construction work is started by putting in the support canes for the four basal stems. It is very unlikely that the tubers have the basal shoots exactly in the right place, so careful consideration has to be given as to where the canes are to be located. It is intended that this plant will have 360° viewing, so the canes are placed in such a way that by tying the shoots to the canes, the shoots can be pulled outwards to open up the centre of the plant. Also the canes will need to be concealed when the foliage and blooms open up. The first cane is taken and placed against one of the chosen outer basal shoots, and remembering where the tuber is, the cane is pushed into the compost until it hits the bottom of the pot. The cane needs to be leaning outwards slightly, so that the shoot can be pulled outwards. If you are not certain where the tuber is, a knitting needle can be carefully probed into the compost to avoid sticking a cane through the tuber. This process is repeated for the other two outer basal shoots.

The fourth basal stem needs to be pulled into the centre of the pot, so some scaffolding is required. A couple of pieces of thinner cane are tied horizontally between two of the basal support canes at different heights, one at about 6in (15cm) above the rim of the pot and the other about 10in (25cm) above the rim of the pot. The two basal support canes are selected so that the two horizontal canes pull the

This pot shows 360° viewing. Note how the leaves extend up to and below the top edge of the plant pot.

A pot about fifty-four days before the show date. Note the leaves are down to the top of the pot. The canes for the basal stems are already in position.

This picture clearly shows one of the basal stem canes and also shows how the basal stem is slowly being pulled outwards to open the pot out.

fourth basal stem in towards the centre of the pot – not all at once, but over the next few weeks. When the plant is fully grown, the foliage should hide all these canes.

Having placed all the canes, the basal stems can be tied to them. Do not try to pull the stems fully back at once. This is done bit by bit over days and weeks, gradually opening up the plant. The fourth basal stem can be gradually pulled towards the centre of the pot by tying it to the lower of the two horizontal canes, positioning it either to the left or to the right, in the centre of the pot. Eventually this can be tied to the top horizontal cane. The shape of the plant is now being constructed. It cannot be stressed firmly enough how important it is to pull the basal stems out gently, bit by bit, over a period of weeks rather than days.

The plant will be growing away quite quickly now. The stems are getting thicker and they will need constantly adjusting and retying. The feeding regime is the same as for growing cut blooms, that is, Chempak No 2 fed at half the recommended strength every other watering. This will give the plant a boost. The emphasis is on the nitrogen to promote growth. A week or so before selecting the buds that are to be flowered (see below), switch to giving a couple of feeds higher in phosphates such

as N:P:K 15:30:15. This will harden the root system. Unless there is a pot full of roots, whether growing for a cut bloom or pot plant, the plant will not reach its full potential. Growing a pot plant needs a lot of care and dedication, but it is well worth the reward when the pot comes into bloom.

With the cut bloom programme there was a fixed show date to work back from. If it is intended to show pot plants, a similar programme is necessary, working back from the show date. Even if not showing it is still worthwhile having a programme of action points. With a pot plant there are a set number of days before certain things should be done, these should be marked on the calendar.

Fifty-four days prior to the show, all flower buds are removed from the plants. There is plenty of time for the plant to develop buds from which the flowering buds will be selected.

Thirty-five to forty days prior to the show, all buds bigger than 1⅛in (30mm) are removed from the plants. The bud stick can be used to check bud sizes. A range of days is given because depending on what variety of flower is being grown, the number of days from the flower bud to fully open bloom will vary. For example, two varieties that take about

The flower buds are starting to poke through the foliage and the stems are thickening nicely. This is about twenty-eight days out and the plant has been stopped.

'Mrs E. McLauchlan' about a fortnight before the show. This pot has a leaf that is intruding into the centre of the plant.

thirty-five days from flower bud to bloom are 'Jessie Cruikshank' and 'Lancelot', whereas 'Apricot Delight' and 'Coppelia' would require about forty days from flower bud to bloom. As a rule of thumb

This plant is about twenty-one days out and some of the leaves have been removed and the halo is starting to form. Bloom supports are being put into position.

the more layers of petals a flower carries, the longer it will take from bud to bloom. Varieties with fewer petals will open more quickly.

Twenty-eight days prior to the show, all the growing tips from the main stems and side shoots are removed. Remember, we are aiming for two flower buds on each of the four main stems and two flower buds on each side shoot coming off these stems. The feed is now changed from a high phosphate feed to a fertilizer with the emphasis on potash to enhance the growth and quality of the bloom. This feed should be done at every second watering at a quarter of the manufacturer's recommended strength. Do not overfeed. Now is the time to insert the bloom supports. Before inserting the telescopic bloom supports, ensure that the supports extend easily and have not stuck together, to avoid ripping off a bloom head when trying to adjust a support. Some of the buds will be over 2in (5cm) now so it can be seen where to place the supports. This part of the job requires lots of patience. Take plenty of time to avoid piercing the tuber or making any small holes in the leaves. When the blooms are big

The same plant with the offending leaf removed.

The same plant of 'Mrs E. McLauchlan' six days before the show. The blooms are being moved to fill the space where the leaf was removed.

enough, remove the two small flower buds that are growing at the back of the chosen male buds. A small pair of pointed scissors is ideal for the job. The plant is growing well now: the leaves are getting larger; the stems are thickening; the buds are getting bigger and starting to open. It is an exciting time.

Twenty-one days prior to the show, it is time to remove all the leaves that appear above the second bud on the main stems and side shoots. This will leave plenty of room for the flowers to spread out and form a halo. Some, if not all, the stems will have to be retied and pulled into a better position. The flower supports will have to be looked at daily and adjusted if necessary. By now the pot will be starting to look more mature. The flowers will be developing nicely and all the hard work is starting to be rewarded.

Fifteen or sixteen days prior to the show, the last important job is to remove all leaves that are obscuring the flowers. These should be cut off carefully as close to the stems as possible.

All that is left to do until the show day is to keep monitoring the plant and checking the final tweaks and adjustments. A good sharp pair of secateurs is a good tool for cutting canes when tidying up the

plants. A very useful tool to have when growing either pot plants or cut blooms is a turntable. The plant can be turned easily when being worked on and also viewed from all angles.

Getting pot plants to a show in good condition is difficult. The sheer size of a well-grown multi-stemmed pot plant is a daunting prospect and it is

Plant almost ready for the show bench. Note: the bloom supports and canes should be unobtrusive.

Pots of 'Ziggy' waiting to be taken to the show. Note the Dacron packed in around the flowers. Dacron does not absorb moisture so the blooms remain dry.

'George McCormick' ready for the show and at the show.

heavy. Flowers need to be firmly fixed to supports and each bloom needs to be wrapped in Dacron (see illustration). Another method is to drape a light-weight net curtain over the plant, which will help to prevent the blooms from moving. To transport the plant it needs to be seated on a flat surface. Wooden boxes can be made with custom made holes into which the pots are seated, or old milk crates can be similarly modified. Whichever method is used, the pots must be firmly wedged in so that they cannot move about. An estate car is fine to transport a few pots, but with more pots it may be necessary to hire a van. Be sure to drive carefully, avoiding sudden stops and starts, and watching out for speed bumps. The prize monies might not cover the expense, but the feeling you get if and when you are awarded a prize card is fantastic.

Here are some of the things a judge will look for:

- The first thing to make sure of is that the plants do not have any disease or pests. This is really common sense more than anything else, and it is only fair to the other competitors.
- Do not show a plant in a dirty pot. A quick wipe down of the outside of the pot with a wet cloth only takes a minute.
- Judges will be looking for a plant that is well grown and has no visible damage. The majority of faults can be rectified before a plant is taken to the show. If there are a couple of damaged blooms, remove them before going to the show.
- Judges will look for other faults such as yellowing leaves, marked leaves, drooping leaves or flowers, flowers that are past their best, or damaged flowers. They will essentially be looking for a well-grown plant with a good show of clean fresh blooms and healthy leaves all the way down the plant. Give your plant a really thorough inspection trying not to deceive yourself and then you won't be deceiving the judges either.

It may be necessary to have a few black painted blocks to place under pots in order to adjust the heights of plants making a group display more attractive.

Check your show schedule to make sure you don't fall into the N.A.S. trap ('not as schedule'). It's easily done and many have suffered for the sake of a last check!

Have a good look at other entries in the class and seek advice from more experienced growers. You will be surprised at the help they will give to you. It is a daunting proposition to enter a competition at a flower show, but everybody likes to admire the flowers, and the amount of satisfaction that you get by seeing your pot on the show bench makes it all worthwhile.

Winning entry – three pots of double tuberous begonias.

CHAPTER 6

Growing pendulas

A magnificent basket of 'Crystal Cascade'.

Pendula begonias are tuberous begonias that have been bred to produce multiple long, weak stems and side shoots, so that the weight of the foliage and blooms will cause the plant to droop down over the sides of a basket or container.

As with the large-flowered tuberous begonias, there are special named varieties of pendula tuberous begonias available from specialist nurseries. These are considerably more expensive than varieties obtainable from garden centres but are altogether in a different class, with flowers of superior shape and form, and given a bit more time and attention these are the varieties that produce the magnificent baskets that win at the shows. There are nowhere near as many named varieties as there are with the large-flowered tuberous begonias, but the popularity of pendula begonias is growing and hybridizing for new, improved varieties seems to be on the increase. Scented pendula tuberous begonias are also available.

Here is a short list of named varieties of pendula begonias that will give good results when grown in baskets or containers:

- 'Firedance' – a beautifully shaped orange flower with great form, and when fully grown it is absolutely magnificent.
- 'Lou-Anne' – a lovely rose-pink flower which

has been around for a few years and is still winning at the shows.

- 'Isabella' – very floriferous with nicely shaped flowers of creamy yellow.
- 'Yellow Sweetie' – a pale lemon with an added attraction of a delicate perfume.
- 'Ophelia' – creamy-white with large flowers.
- 'Champagne' – the name depicts its colour, very floriferous.

Other types of pendula tuberous begonias, which are available at most garden centres, will give a superb colourful show in a basket or other type of container and are excellent value for money. These pendula begonias can be bought as seed, tubers or as plantlets. Often the tubers will have names but these should not be confused with the special named varieties described above. Begonia 'Illumination' plugs or plantlets and similar types are available in separate colours at most garden centres, or can be bought as F1 hybrid seed, and will give a stunning display with three or four plants in a basket, window box or wall planter. One major advantage, as with all begonias, is that they do not need direct sunlight and will give a superb display even on a north wall or under a porch.

One other begonia that can give a superb display when grown in baskets or containers is *Begonia sutherlandii*. This is a species, a naturally occurring begonia, not a hybrid. It is tuberous and produces only small, single orange flowers, but the mass of bloom produced is spectacular (*see* Chapter 8).

Pendula begonia 'Illumination Orange'.

Small bulbils appear in the leaf axils; these can be used for propagation.

Pendula begonias can be grown from seed, but this will not produce sufficient bloom in the first year. Growing from seed is done to produce tubers for general garden use in subsequent years or when trying to develop new hybrids.

Pendula tuberous begonias are usually grown from tubers. To get a large mass of bloom, a large plant is needed. This requires a long growing season so this means the tubers need to be started early. Pendula tubers should be started in a hot bed or propagator any time from the middle of January to the middle of February.

Even at this time consideration should be given to the final basket or container. If growing for a show, notice should be taken of what type of container is specified and how many tubers are allowed; consult the schedule carefully. For showing, usually only baskets are grown and the number of tubers per basket is not specified. As a rough guide, to grow a decent 12in (30cm) basket, three small tubers of 2–3in (5–7.5cm) are required, or two tubers 4–5in (10–12.5cm), or one tuber over 6in (15cm); all the tubers in a basket should be the same variety.

The tubers are started off in the propagator or hot bed as described in Chapter 3. After about four weeks or so, depending somewhat on the temperature, a good root system should have developed. It may be preferred to start the tubers in pots of compost plunged into the hot bed and the tubers

A striking basket of 'Firedance'.

transferred to the basket when the roots reach the edge of the pots. This can give less root disturbance. Once the tubers are growing well and the shoots are about 2½in (6cm) high, it is time to transfer the growing tubers into the hanging basket or container.

If a basket is to be grown, it will be lined with sphagnum moss or a commercial liner from a garden centre. If a plastic liner is used make sure there are drainage holes. Also ensure that the rim of the basket is covered with either moss or the liner to prevent chafing of the stems. If growing a basket for a show, any stipulations in the show schedule must be adhered to.

The basket, or container, is part filled with John Innes No 2 compost. Then very carefully the root balls are lifted from the hot bed or propagator and placed into the prepared basket. Endeavour to keep the surface of the compost at the same level as in the hot box they have been taken from, and position so that the majority of the shoots are pointing towards the edge of the basket. The John Innes No 2 compost is packed around the root balls, leaving a slight depression on the top of the compost, as an aid to watering. Try and have the compost at about the same temperature as the hot box so there is as little shock as possible to the growing tubers. It would be ideal if the basket or container could be placed on the surface of the hot box compost for a day or two before finally weaning it off the heat into the ambient temperature of the greenhouse, which should never be allowed to go lower than 50°F (10°C). Leave the basket overnight before watering, enabling the compost to settle in around the root ball. On the next day lightly water with tepid water.

The aim when growing a basket or container of pendula tuberous begonias is to produce as much bloom as possible. It is not the size of the individual blooms that is important, it is the total mass of bloom that matters. Pendula tuberous begonias are bred to be multi-stemmed and produce plenty of side shoots, thus producing many blooms. Unlike the cut blooms and pot plants previously described, stems and side shoots are not restricted and all the flowers, both male and female, are left on the plant to give the maximum amount of bloom. So if the basket or container as prepared above, is watered and fed regularly, is shaded from direct sunlight whilst in the greenhouse and not put outside until

Top: the plant before the first stop, stems about 6in (15cm) long with ½in (12mm) buds. Bottom: the plant after the first stop. The removed material can be used as cuttings.

early June, with a bit of deadheading a very satisfactory basket should result which will last for several weeks. At the end of the season these tubers can be saved but, unless they were expensive, it is probably easier to buy new stock next year.

However, to get really superb exhibition quality baskets it is necessary to grow the special named

Top: before the second stop. Bottom: after the second stop. Plenty of cuttings have been taken.

The finished basket after the two stops, five months after starting the tuber. The variety is Orange Cascade.

varieties of pendula tubers in a greenhouse. By removing the early flower buds and stopping the plants twice, as described below, the maximum amount of growth and bloom will be obtained.

When the stems are about 6in (15cm) long with three or four leaf joints the first flower buds will appear, and it is time for the first stop. When they are about ½in (12mm) long, the flower buds are removed and the growing tips of the shoots are pinched out. This will cause the side shoots to start growing from the stems.

To obtain a large amount of growth in a limited amount of compost, correct watering and feeding are very important. After the first stopping, the begonias can be sprayed with one of the proprietary leaf feeds. This should be done on dull days to avoid scorching. In general most proprietary peat-based

composts have only enough nutrients to last around four to six weeks before the fertilizers have dissipated (mostly through watering, but also some will have been taken up by the plant). John Innes No 2 will hold the fertilizer slightly longer, but it is essential to start leaf feeding from this early stage to give the plants sufficient nutrients to last until feeding is started into the basket itself.

Two or three weeks after the first stop, the new side shoots will be growing away and possibly some smaller basal shoots emerging. Now is the time to start feeding directly into the basket with a high nitrogen feed such as Chempak No 2. It is better to feed at a quarter of the manufacturer's recommended dosage rate at every watering, rather than watering with a full-strength mix at intervals. There will begin to be a big difference in the baskets now as the nitrogen builds up the stems and side shoots, and the leaves become a lush green colour.

A few weeks later, flower buds will be seen on the new side shoots. When the buds have reached a size of about ½in (12mm) it is time for the second stop. The flower buds are removed and the growing tips pinched out just as before, only this time there will be a lot more tips to remove. After this second stop the feeding regime is changed from high nitrogen feed to high potash feed such as Chempak No 4, again at quarter strength every watering. The high nitrogen feed was to create growth; the high potash feed is to encourage flowering.

After this second stop, even more side shoots are forced into growth. These are the side shoots that will eventually produce the mass of bloom for the show. The baskets will be getting quite large by now. To get even growth around the basket it may be necessary to turn it occasionally. If it is necessary to reposition some of the stems, by withholding water for a couple of days the stems will go limp and can be moved more easily. Check that the basket is not too big to get it through the greenhouse door. If this is going to be the case then consider growing it for the last month in a shade house or a polytunnel.

Timing pendula begonias for a show is not as precise as timing for cut bloom or pot plant begonias, and fortunately it is not so critical. By deadheading old blooms, the succession of new blooms will keep a basket looking superb for several weeks. As a very rough guide and depending upon temperatures, from starting off a tuber to the first stop can take eight weeks, from the first stop to the second stop can be seven weeks, and from the second stop to a basket in full bloom can be up to ten weeks, totalling almost six months from start to finish. Starting and stopping dates should be recorded so that if they don't work out they can be adjusted for subsequent years.

The aim when showing is to produce a basket with as much fresh bloom as possible. All the flowers, both male and female, are allowed to bloom. Prior to the show remove any flowers that are past their best and also any damaged leaves. Finally make a note of anything that might improve results for the next year.

Transporting a hanging basket to a show is difficult. It can be 3ft across, 2ft deep and a considerable weight. The basket can be hung during transportation and tethered to prevent it swinging about. Or it can be placed on top of a large heavy plant pot that has been securely wedged. It is possible to make a special carrying frame where the basket is placed in the top and the pendula stems are hung down the side. Whatever method is used it is a good idea to drape a lightweight net curtain over the whole plant to prevent the blooms from moving about too much. It is impractical to try and protect each bloom with cotton wool. Allow plenty of time to get to the show and try to drive carefully, but it is inevitable that a few blooms will be lost.

At the show there will be a framework from which

'Firedance' and 'Isabella' grown as a tower.

There is just one tuber in this basket. Water has been withheld so the stems became lax and can be repositioned if necessary.

the hanging basket can be suspended, or basket stands may be provided upon which the basket is placed. Either way the basket will be displayed at or slightly above head height. Ensure that there is adequate time to get the staging cards and arrange the basket. Give a final watering. Check one last time; after that it is all up to the judges.

Propagation of named varieties of pendula begonias is by basal or axil cuttings, as described in Chapter 11. However, taking basal or axil cuttings will reduce the amount of growth from a tuber and consequently the amount of bloom. One way to minimize this problem is at the first stop to cut some

of the longer stems below a leaf joint and use these as cuttings. But perhaps a better way is to grow one tuber of each variety as a stock plant solely for taking cuttings.

At the end of the season the plants are treated as described in Chapter 3. Around the end of September the growing stems are stopped, the plant is watered less frequently, and over October and November allowed to die back. When the tubers are harvested at the end of the year, it will be found that they have considerably increased in size so that they will throw up more shoots and give even bigger and better baskets the following year.

Pendula and multiflora begonias.

CHAPTER 7

Growing outdoors

'Le Flamboyant' multiflora begonia in a wheelbarrow.

The begonias described here refer to tuberous begonias that are grown for flowering outside in the garden in flowerbeds or containers, and include 'Non Stop' and 'multiflora' begonias. *Begonia semperflorens*, a very commonly used bedding plant, is a fibrous rooted begonia, not a tuberous begonia, and so is not described here.

If the begonias are to be planted in beds in the garden, the soil needs to be well dug to give good drainage, and plenty of organic material should be

incorporated. The pH can be tested and if necessary a light dressing of dolomite lime can be used to sweeten the soil, as begonias do not like to grow in too acid a condition. The site of a bed for begonias ideally should not be exposed to constant sunshine especially at midday, but on the other hand it should not be in perpetual deep shade. Prior to planting, a dressing of general purpose fertilizer should be applied. If the begonias are to be planted in containers, multipurpose or John Innes No 2 compost should be used with an occasional application of liquid fertilizer.

If it is the intention at the end of the growing season that the tubers will be saved for the following year, it is important that the plants are treated to resist attack by vine weevil. The systemic insecticides imidacloprid and thiacloprid can be used to treat plants while growing in pots prior to being planted outside.

LARGE-FLOWERED BEGONIAS

Large-flowered tuberous double begonias can be flowered in the garden but these will not normally be the named varieties, which would be far too expensive for this purpose. Un-named begonia tubers in separate colours (scarlet, crimson, pink, orange, yellow, cream, white, bicolour and picotee) are available from nurseries and garden centres at reasonable prices, as are coloured fimbriata begonia tubers (highly frilled petals) and some single-flowered begonia tubers. Seeds are available from the major seed suppliers, and plantlets of various types are available in springtime.

The seeds or the tuberous begonia tubers can be started into growth in January or February, as described in Chapter 3. Plantlets, usually obtainable in April, will need to be potted on and grown in the greenhouse until it is time to harden them off. When growing for outside bedding, the number of stems and side shoots is not normally restricted.

After hardening off, preferably in a cold frame, the plants can be put outside in early June. The planting distance between large flowered tuberous begonias is 12–15in (30–38cm) depending upon the size of the tubers. It is also possible to plant tubers directly into the ground in late April or early May. By this time the tubers will be showing some shoots but so long as the tops of the tubers are 2in (5cm) below soil level they should have protection against any late frosts. Staking is usually required, and a liquid feed now and again will be beneficial. The female flowers are not usually removed, giving the maximum amount of bloom. Flowers on plants grown outside are generally more brightly coloured than flowers grown in a shaded greenhouse.

Around the middle of September, or after the first frost has blackened the leaves, any plants that are to be saved for the following year should be brought into the greenhouse and allowed to die back and the tubers stored (as described in Chapter 3).

Some exhibitors, who prefer to use the larger two-year or older tubers of named variety begonias to grow cut blooms, will flower the one-year-old cutting tubers outside in a raised bed. After starting the cutting tubers in the greenhouse and potting up

Named varieties in the garden.

into 5in or 6in (12.5cm or 15cm) pots, at the beginning of June after hardening off, the whole pot is plunged into the raised bed. The plants are allowed to flower all summer giving a colourful display in the garden. In September, well before any frosts, the pots are lifted and brought back into the greenhouse, allowed to die back and stored as described in Chapter 3.

NON STOP BEGONIAS

Of the tuberous begonias the most often used as bedding plants are the 'Non Stops'. Over recent years there have been considerable improvements with Non Stop begonias and they are now widely used by local authorities in mass bedding schemes for parks and gardens. As the name indicates, Non Stop begonias will flower all summer long and they are equally suitable for either sunny or semi-shaded areas. There is a wide range of flower colours, and as well as the normal green foliage there are 'Mocca' varieties with chocolate foliage.

Non Stop begonias can be grown from F1 hybrid seed purchased from the major seed merchants; plug plants and plantlets are available; alternatively, tubers saved from the previous year can also be used. Seeds sown in late December to early January can be expected to start flowering in June or July. Again, growing of seed, plantlets or tubers is as described in Chapter 3 except that the plants are hardened off in May and planted out in June.

Tubers can be planted directly in the ground in late April or early May. Non Stop begonias grow to a height of 8–10in (20–25cm) and need to be spaced 6–8in (15–20cm) apart. Staking is not required and all stems are allowed to grow. Blooms will be about 3in (7.5cm) across and the female flowers are not removed. With some deadheading and an occasional feed, non-stop begonias should give continual flowering from late June until mid-September.

If the tubers are to be kept for the following year they should be dug up in late September and brought into the greenhouse, allowed to dry off, and the tubers stored, again as described in Chapter 3.

Non Stop begonias are sometimes used at flower shows in flowerbed competitions, often between local authorities.

MULTIFLORA BEGONIAS

Multiflora begonias have small flowers up to 2in (5cm) across, which can be either single or double depending on the variety. As the name suggests, the plants bear a great number of flowers. Plant heights range from 4in (10cm) to around 9in (23cm), with spacing 6–9in (15–23cm) or more with large tubers.

All multiflora begonias are named varieties and must be propagated vegetatively, which makes them relatively more expensive than Non Stop begonias, which can be raised from seed. In the past many varieties were available, but only a few have survived to the present day. Fortunately, there has been a recent renewal of interest in multiflora begonias and

Non Stop begonia 'Mocca Scarlet'.

'Madame Richard Gallé'.

A plantlet of the multiflora begonia 'Peardrops'.

new varieties are now coming on the market. Probably the best known of the older varieties that are still grown is 'Le Flamboyant'. This has brilliant bright scarlet single flowers with a yellow centre and when mass planted is absolutely stunning. Suitable for beds, borders, tubs, containers, and hanging baskets, 'Le Flamboyant' grows to about 9in (23cm) in height and will flower continuously from June through to September. Another older variety still available is 'Madame Richard Gallé', a semi-double yellow variety.

Plantlets of the named varieties of multiflora begonias are available around April time from specialized nurseries. These should be transplanted into pots and kept in the greenhouse and gradually hardened off for planting out in early June. Remove the first flower buds: this will make a larger plant with more flowers later. Multiflora begonias are susceptible to mildew so must not be allowed to dry out. Spray with a suitable fungicide at the first sign of any attack.

After the first frost, the plants can be lifted, brought into the greenhouse and allowed to die back. The small tubers can be stored and used the following year. After a few years the tubers can get quite large. Propagation is by these tubers or by small basal cuttings pulled off the tubers during the growing season. With the newer varieties it is important to check the plant label: if the variety claims Plant Breeders' Rights it is illegal to propagate that variety without a licence.

There is not usually a specific competitive class for multiflora begonias at flower shows, but plants in containers can be entered in a general class such as 'Begonia in flower' or 'One Pot Plant Begonia not specified elsewhere in the schedule'.

SPECIES

Species are naturally occurring begonias. As well as *Begonia sutherlandii* (*see* Chapter 6), there are two other species of tuberous begonias that are often grown outside. *Begonia gracilis martiniana*, the hollyhock begonia, grows a single upright stem about 24in (60cm) high bearing pink flowers. *Begonia grandis* grows up to 24in high bearing pink or white flowers. It is just about hardy in the south of the UK and the tubers can be left in the ground over the winter period. Propagation of all three of these species is by cuttings or the tiny bulbils that form in the leaf axils.

There are some other types of begonias suitable for growing outside, which can be obtained from garden centres or by mail order. These will have a descriptive name and are invariably bought as growing plants but are in fact tuberous begonias and the tuber can be kept to grow the following year. (Note, however, that if the label on the plant claims Plant Breeders' Rights it is illegal to propagate that variety without a licence.)

CHAPTER 8

Varieties to grow

This chapter contains pictures of some of my favourite flowers. Some are old favourites that you will recognize straight away and some are newer varieties that you may not have seen. One thing you may be assured of is that they are all very desirable and would grace any greenhouse. The majority of the photographs were taken in my greenhouse with one or two exceptions that were taken in a friend's greenhouse or at a show.

The number of varieties that are grown is amazing. It would appear that begonia varieties are similar to ladies' fashions: in one year and out the next year! This is good for growers as it enables us to try new varieties and different colours, but be warned not to be too hasty when discarding old varieties. Some varieties included in these next few pages have been around for a long time and are still favourites today.

The colour classification is taken from the National Begonia Society website register. This shows the correct colour class on a show schedule. For example, with cut bloom classes:

Class 1: three reds
Class 2: three blooms picotee or bicolour
Class 8: three yellow or cream

These classifications allow the exhibitor to place the blooms into the correct classes. Read your show schedule closely; if you are in doubt ask another competitor.

The National Begonia Society has yet to classify the colours of some of the newer varieties. In the following pages, the colour classification for these is given as ————.

'Anne Crawford', raised by the legendary George McCormick. One of the best yellows around, with lovely coloured wavy petals and a terrific shape. George raised so many really great cultivars during his lifetime that his name will be remembered, and the blooms he produced will still be grown for many years. Colour classification: yellow.

'Bernat Klein', yet another variety from Blackmore & Langdon. This has been around for quite a while; it is a very good white with thick petals that look almost like parchment. This variety is a tall grower and can grow to quite a large size. Of all the whites this one is the most reliable as a cut bloom. Colour classification: white.

'Avalanche', raised by Blackmore & Langdon and introduced in 1971. This is a truly magnificent bloom: it has size, shape and form with layers of wonderful wavy petals. It is probably still as much sought after now as it was when it was released. For the show board there is none better. Colour classification: white.

'Dr Eric Catterall', a beautiful bloom raised by the well-known begonia grower Robert Bryce. It was named after the late secretary of the National Begonia Society. The bloom is a magnificent red with layer after layer of wavy petals. It has a camellia centre and is popular with growers. This is yet another fine example of amateur hybridizing. Colour classification: ————.

'George McCormick', the variety that was named after one of the best ever hybridizers. It is a beautiful white picotee with a heavy red edge. This variety produces a really good pot plant and an excellent cut bloom, and it will brighten up any greenhouse. Colour classification: white picotee.

'Goliath' is yet another introduction from Blackmore & Langdon. Described as a large tomato red, it certainly lives up to its name. It is reliable, propagates easily and can grow to a very large size. This is a cut bloom variety and is still very much sought after by show enthusiasts. Colour classification: red.

'George Tatton', named after the man who raised it. During his life George raised thousands of seedlings (one of which he named 'Louise Kimber' after his granddaughter). This latest variety may very well prove to be the best he ever raised. This bloom was named by Mr D. Hague after George died, so, sadly, he never knew what a magnificent beautiful bloom he had produced. Colour classification: orange.

'Icemint' is a new variety raised by Margaret Watson of Bellcross Nurseries. It was named in 2007 and is a white bloom with a greenish/yellow centre. It has a lovely rosebud centre and I think we will see more of this variety grown as pot plants as well as cut blooms. Colour classification: ———.

'Isobel Keenan'. This variety was introduced by the well-known Scottish grower Bill Dodds. It is a startlingly bright bloom that would set off anyone's board. It grows large, well-shaped blooms, has a nice rosebud centre and is popular at the shows. Colour classification: white picotee.

'Jessie Cruickshank' has been around for some time. It was raised by George McCormick and named after his friend Bert Cruickshank's wife Jessie. This has been a very popular pot plant and has been 'best pot' in show on many occasions, very reliable. Colour classification: white picotee.

'Joyce Mihulka': when I first saw this bloom at Ayr I thought it was the nicest bloom that I had ever seen: it seemed to come alive as you were looking at it. It is big and it is beautiful. Colour classification:————.

'Kathryn Hartley' is a sport of 'Roy Hartley'. It sported for Margaret Watson of Bellcross Nurseries in 1971. It has proved to be a very popular cultivar and makes an excellent pot plant as well as a very good cut bloom. Its colour I find hard to describe: it reminds me of an oyster colour. In 1979, 'Kathryn Hartley' itself sported to give a creamy-white coloured begonia, which was named 'Ann Hartley'. The three varieties, Roy, Kathryn and Ann, are like peas in a pod except for their different colours. Colour classification: pink.

'Laura Gardiner', a cultivar raised by the well-known Scottish grower and hybridizer John Hamilton and named after one of his relatives. I have been growing this variety for a number of years and now seem to have got the hang of it. It is big, bright red, and has a lovely rosebud centre. It looks great on an exhibition board. Colour classification: red.

'Linda Jackson' is a very distinctive plant, recognized easily by its pale green foliage. It was raised by George Jackson. It is a tall grower and carries a superb flower. It is good as a cut bloom and I have seen it when it has been successful as a pot plant. If you are looking for a good red you need look no further. Colour classification: red.

'Lyndsay Murray' is yet another begonia from Scotland. It is a very fine-edged yellow picotee. This bloom is shown a lot in Scotland. One particularly attractive feature is its very fine picotee edging. Colour classification: ———.

'Mary Heatley', perhaps my own favourite. In 1968 it was described as a warm shade of golden orange. It was raised by Blackmore & Langdon, and in 1968 would have cost the princely sum of £2.50. It has been around for forty years and will doubtless be sought after in another forty years. Colour classification: orange.

'Mia', one of the newer arrivals from Blackmore & Langdon. The petal shape is slightly unusual as is the background colour, completed by a beautiful rosebud centre. Colour classification: ————.

'Monica Bryce' was raised by Alan Bryce and was named after his mother. It has all the required qualities of form, shape, good colour and best of all a beautiful rosebud centre. It is amongst the most popular yellows shown today. Colour classification: yellow.

'Mrs Elizabeth McLauchlan' is a cultivar that seems to have been around for ever. It propagates easily and is both an excellent pot plant and a superb cut bloom. This is without doubt the easiest variety for a novice to grow well. Its raiser was none other than George McCormick. Colour classification: bicolour.

'Mrs Elizabeth McLauchlan' shown as a pot plant. It throws up plenty of flowers and is very eye-catching. The size and number of blooms on this pot are quite amazing. When comparing the colour of this and the picture (left), it must be noted that the pot is shown under artificial light, whereas the cut bloom is in natural greenhouse light.

'Nichola Coates' was raised by the well-known amateur hybridizer Dave Coates, and named after his daughter. It grows easily to size and is a beautiful salmon pink with a camellia centre. This variety often wins best bloom in show and is one variety that I would not be without. Colour classification: pink.

'Robert Tyler Murphy Bryce', one of Bob Bryce's new varieties named after his son. A beautiful bloom with a rosebud centre, it grows to a very large size without losing its shape or form and will certainly be much sought after. Colour classification: ———.

'Powder Puff', a variety raised by Harry Bridges. This is a very good pale pink bloom, which was very popular when it first appeared. It produces beautiful flowers of very good size and shape with that desirable rosebud centre. Colour classification: pink.

'Roy Hartley', another very fine cultivar from Blackmore & Langdon who introduced it in about 1961, and it is still as popular as ever. When this bloom is grown correctly and in the right light, its colour is almost fluorescent. All in all it is a magnificent bloom. Colour classification: pink.

'**Ruby Young**', one of the finest blooms I have ever seen and have had the pleasure of growing. It was raised by an excellent grower on the Scottish borders by the name of Rob Young. Sadly he is no longer with us and so will never know how popular it has become. It is both a good pot plant and also excellent as a cut bloom. Colour classification: ————.

'**Ruby Young**' (pot plant), not quite ready for showing and yet you can see the potential already. This pot will be absolutely magnificent on the day. The halo will be huge and the beautiful green foliage comes right down to the top of the pot. I feel sure that this variety will be on the show benches for years to come. Colour classification: ————.

'**Suzanne Redmayne**' was raised by an amateur grower from Blackburn in 1983, Fred Walsh, who produced some really superb blooms. This one is a nice soft orange and grows to a very large size, which is ideal for any cut bloom growers. Colour classification: orange.

'**Sweet Dreams**': a must for cut bloom growers. Introduced in 1975 by Blackmore & Langdon, it has been with us for a long time. A beautiful clean pink, it is one of the most popular pinks grown today. Colour classification: pink.

'**Tom Brownlee**', a variety raised by George McCormick, and certainly the most popular red on the cut bloom show bench. It grows to an enormous size with layer upon layer of petals and takes a long time to open fully, but the wait is worth it. Superb as a cut bloom but not so good as a pot plant. Colour classification: red.

'**Westlawn Tango**', a beautiful bloom raised by Mr Derek Foster. It grows to a very large size and has many layers of beautiful orange petals. Derek Foster also released another two cultivars, 'Westlawn Carousel' (a frilly light orange) and 'Westlawn Jill' (red). Colour classification: orange.

'**Whispers**', raised by an amateur grower, Dave Staines. The variety has only been around for a few years and is already making an impact on the show boards. It is one of those few varieties that make a tremendous pot plant and a fabulous cut bloom. This plant will be around for a long time to come. Colour classification: cream.

'**White Bali Hi**'. (The only Bali Hi in the register is a yellow Bali Hi; it must have sported somewhere along the line to a white variety.) If you can catch this bloom at its peak you have a real winner, but unfortunately it does not stay at its best for very long. Colour classification: yellow picotee.

A new seedling, raised by Robert Bryce. One for the future, perhaps?

A new seedling, raised by Alan Bryce. Another one for the future?

'Isabella' must be one of the most beautifully formed pendulas available today. Its gorgeous creamy yellow flowers cascade freely. This variety is very floriforous and will require frequent feeding throughout the flowering period.

'Lou-Anne', one of the older pendula varieties that is still a favourite. The colour is a very attractive pink and it is very floriferous. This variety is one of the more popular varieties seen on the show benches, especially in Scotland.

Begonia sutherlandii. This is not a hybrid but a species begonia from South Africa. To say that it is floriforous would be an understatement, and the pale orange colour is very attractive. If you do decide to grow this variety, ensure that you spray it well for mildew. At the back end of the season you can dry off the seed pods, store the seeds and the following spring you will be able to cultivate dozens of new plants.

Non Stop 'Mocca Orange', 'Mocca Yellow' and 'Mocca Scarlet' in a bedding arrangement. Perhaps the most popular of all the bedding begonias.

'Le Flamboyant' is usually grown as a bedding plant; planted in a sunny spot one would be hard pressed to find something with more colour. Grown as a hanging basket it is also stunning: the colour is absolutely vibrant. It is easy to cultivate and can also be used in window boxes or simply planted into pots. This one is an absolute must-have.

'Yellow Hammer', a beautiful bright yellow multiflora bedding variety, which can also be grown as a pot plant or in a basket.

CHAPTER 9

Flower shows

The beginnings of competition at flower shows or horticultural shows started when plant collecting from exotic foreign parts became all the rage and the landed gentry started showing off their acquisitions to their friends. In the early part of the nineteenth century horticultural societies started up and, along with commercial nurseries and the Royal Botanic Gardens at Kew, started sponsoring more plant-hunting trips. Shows were organized to act as a marketplace for the commercial nurseries to show their new plants and hybrids, and this continues to the present day.

The middle and working classes started taking an interest in horticulture, and the growing of particular plants was often undertaken on a regional basis. Roses, carnations and sweet peas were popular in Cumbria and the Lake District, while in Northumberland and the North East, growers favoured leeks, onions and vegetables (and many still do). Dahlias and chrysanthemums were commonly grown in Lancashire, Yorkshire, Staffordshire and the Midlands. In the southern part of England fruit growing was particularly popular. Horticultural societies were no longer just for the wealthy, and keen gardeners started to form local horticultural societies. Societies varied in size from

Interested spectators at the Ayr Flower Show.

the local village society right up to the nation-wide Royal Horticultural Society. After the 1845 General Enclosure Act, allotments became available for the working class and consequently Allotment Societies came into being.

The first UK plant societies were set up in the latter half of the nineteenth century. These included the national societies for chrysanthemums (1846), carnations (1850), auriculas (1872), roses (1876), dahlias (1881) and daffodils (1898). Begonias were scarcely known at this time and it was much later that the various begonia societies were established. The American Begonia Society was formed in 1932. There was a lot of interest in growing begonias in Scotland and the Scottish Begonia Society was founded in 1936. The National Begonia Society (covering all the United Kingdom except Scotland) was formed in 1948.

The written constitution of these societies almost always included the establishment of an annual show or exhibition. These usually had a competitive element. Thus, throughout the country there were, and still are, hundreds, if not thousands, of annual flower shows. Also there were the town shows and the county shows, and although these were not primarily horticultural shows, they usually contained a competitive horticultural section. Shrewsbury Flower Show is claimed to be the world's longest running horticultural show, established in 1875.

When it comes to amateur competition there are big differences between the small horticultural shows and the large horticultural shows. The small, local shows consist entirely of competitive exhibits grown by amateurs, perhaps alongside handicraft and cookery competitions. With the large shows, competitive amateur exhibits are usually only a small part of the show. At the Royal Horticultural Society shows and one or two other large shows there are no amateur competitive exhibits, although plant societies are sometimes allowed to put on a small non-competitive promotional display.

EXHIBITING AT A SHOW

Having grown tuberous begonias and appreciating what fabulous plants and flowers they are, the urge may come to show off what you can achieve and exhibit at one of the flower shows. In the United Kingdom, tuberous begonias usually flower between the end of June and the end of September. Flower shows that cater for tuberous begonias are from mid-July to early September.

You may prefer to begin showing at a small, local show. Many villages and local districts will have a horticultural society that organizes an annual flower show. In a small show you may be lucky enough to find a class for 'one begonia in flower'. Failing that, the class to enter may just read 'one plant in bloom'. There will be classes for flowering plants, and possibly a class for baskets, but there will not be any classes for cut blooms of begonias. The classes may be 'open', that is, open to non-members of the society. Small shows will last for just one day, perhaps with staging (arranging the exhibits) in the morning, judging around lunchtime, open to the public in the afternoon and finishing with the prize-giving. The prize money is likely to be miniscule but there may be a trophy. However, the excitement of showing and the pleasure of getting a winning card, usually red, make it all worthwhile.

One or two of the larger shows do have open classes for exhibiting begonias but exhibits are few and tend not to be of a high standard. Joining a begonia society is the best way to progress in growing and showing begonias, and essential if you want to exhibit cut blooms. In the United Kingdom there are the Scottish Begonia Society, covering Scotland, and the National Begonia Society, covering the rest of the United Kingdom and Ireland. Membership fees are very modest and members receive a handbook and regular colour bulletins. The societies are concerned with promoting and encouraging the cultivation of all types of begonias, not just tuberous begonias. Both societies organize area meetings and area shows, and both societies have one annual national show.

Joining a society will allow you to meet people with the same interests in growing begonias. It is the only way to find out about the latest varieties, many of which are raised by amateurs. Friendships are formed at the meetings and shows. Tubers and plants can be bought or exchanged, and advice and information on growing begonias is readily given. Other growers' greenhouses can be visited. New members to either of the societies are made very

Arriving at the show.

welcome. Exhibitors are the driving force of the societies, so potential exhibitors are especially encouraged. Most begonia growers, whether exhibitors or not, will be members of one or even both of the societies.

Whether showing at a local show, at a begonia society show or at a large show, the method of entering an exhibit is the same. The first thing to do is to apply to the show secretary for a copy of the show schedule and an entry form. The show schedule is usually a booklet containing all the information and instructions for exhibiting at the show; the whole document should be read very carefully. Probably of primary interest will be the schedule of classes to determine which of the classes to enter. There will be an entry form included, and a last date for entries stipulated. At a local show entries may be accepted on the morning of the show. For each class entered there will usually be an entry fee.

As well as details of the classes, entry forms and entry fees, the schedule should contain all the other information needed for exhibiting at a show. The staging times will be stated, as will details of where

to park when staging. The names of the judges will be given and the times for judging as well as prize money and perhaps trophies for each of the classes. There will also be procedures for taking back exhibits at the end of the show. It is important to read the show schedule very carefully to make sure all the rules are complied with. If you are uncertain about anything in the schedule, try and contact someone who has previously exhibited at that show.

Having decided that you can meet all the criteria in the schedule, the entry form should be filled in and sent along with the relevant fees to the show secretary to arrive before the closing date for entries. Procedures do vary between the shows, but you are likely to receive a letter thanking you for entering the show and informing you that there will be an envelope waiting for you at the show with the appropriate documents and staging instructions that you will require. You may even receive a parking ticket enabling you to park near the show tent while unloading your exhibit.

After sending in the entry form, if you find that you are unable to provide an exhibit, the show administrator should be informed as soon as possible. Failure to turn up without prior notification as a matter of courtesy may even result in a ban from future shows. On the other hand, once you exhibit at a show you are likely to be invited to show again the following year and be sent a schedule and entry form without having to apply for them.

When you arrive at the showground at the designated staging time, you will need to seek out the steward and request your staging pack. This will contain your entry classes, bloom name cards, class numbers and an entry ticket to the show. If the show lasts for more than one day, there will also be a 'lifting ticket' so that at the end of the show you can enter the show ground to remove your exhibit.

Again there will be strict rules on times and parking to avoid congestion.

Finally, find out where the classes entered are to be staged and display your exhibit. Make sure you have followed the schedule instructions to the letter. The worst thing that can happen, after all the work that goes into an exhibit, is to be disqualified with an N.A.S. (not as schedule) scribbled by the judge on your entry card, or even scrawled on the table cover – very deflating and a real 'put down'!

BEGONIA SOCIETY SHOWS

As already stated, by far the best way to exhibit tuberous begonias is to join one of the begonia

---

JUDGING RULES FOR BEGONIAS

This is a summary of the National Begonia Society's general rules for the judging of begonias. These rules apply to the judging of all types of tuberous begonia, whether flowering plants or cut blooms.

Freshness
1. Flowers and foliage should appear fresh with no edging to either flowers or foliage.
2. Flowers should be facing forwards, not upright or drooping.
3. Back petals should be showing no signs of scorching.
4. All petals should be present with no signs of trimming or petal removal.

Diseases
1. Mildew. Any plant showing visible signs of mildew should be removed by the stewards from the show bench and not judged. The exhibitor should be diplomatically informed that it could be spread to other exhibitors' plants.
2. The judges will be alert to stem rot due to poor cultivation, and will mark down accordingly.

Quality: flowering plants
1. Flowers should be symmetrical in shape.
2. Multiple centres should not be present in any flowers.
3. Flowers should be equally spaced around the plant, not overlapping each other.
4. The plant should be in balance.
5. The top of the plant should preferably be full with flowers, not openly spaced.
6. Colour run or blotching should be avoided if possible; points will be lost if present.
7. Leaves should not be marked or yellowing.
8. Foliage should commence at the pot level with no bare stems showing the removal of foliage.
9. The size of the majority of flowers on the plant should be commensurate with the variety. Judges should take into consideration exceptional sizes of flowers known to be normally small, and should judge accordingly.
10. Each main stem should preferably be carrying side shoots, with at least one flower, which should be fully open. The main stem should preferably be carrying three flowers.
11. Picotee edging should be sharp and clear.

Quality: cut blooms
1. Blooms should not contain any blemishes.
2. Travel and handling damage should not be present.
3. All petals should be present, with no trimming visible.
4. All blooms should be matched for size.
5. Blooms should be to those dimensions expected of the cultivar.

6. Blooms should be the colour expected of the cultivar.
7. Blooms should have a circular outline.
8. Blooms should have good depth.
9. Blooms should be refined and not coarse in texture (heavy veining of the petals).
10. Warts (undeveloped petals) should not be present.
11. There should be uniformity to the bloom's centre.
12. Separation of the component colour pigments in pastel shades is a fault.

Comments on the rules by Derek Telford, a leading N.B.S. judge

Every exhibit – of whatever flower – should first be examined for form and freshness. These are the paramount requirements in exhibiting begonia blooms or plants. It should be remembered, however, that there has never been an exhibit or a flower without a fault.

Form

- In the case of the double-flowering begonia, 'form' means blooms should be round or symmetrical and have good depth.
- There should be equal placements of the petals so that there aren't any gaps on the periphery of the blooms.
- Warts seem to disfigure the petal placements since they push them apart.
- Multiple centres detract from the form but there is nothing in our rules that requires rosebud centres or requires down-pointing of ovate centres. It is pleasing to see rosebud centres but care has to be taken to ensure that personal preferences are not brought into the judging.
- I have seen the odd concave centre in a bloom or a hole in the middle of a rosebud centre; I believe that this detracts from the symmetry of the bloom. The latter sometimes heralds the 'blowing' of the centre. If the bloom is too old and the centre opens (blows) it will be down-pointed.
- In the case of picotee varieties, the picotee edging should be present on each petal.
- Cut blooms should be matched for size.
- In the case of pot plants, the total form of the plant embraces the placement of the blooms to ensure that each bloom is seen in its entirety and no gap should be left in the centre of the plant. Leaves should not be permitted to obscure the blooms and detract from the general unity and balance.
- The plants should have leaves gracefully produced and covering the lower stems and reaching to and beyond the rim of the pot.
- The standard of excellence should be strived for in the single pot classes with 360° viewing – in spite of being viewed against a tent wall.
- It should be realized that a judge has the duty to inspect plants ensuring that faults are not hidden at the rear of the exhibits. This is not possible in the case of group displays.
- In the case of our classes of three-, six-, or seven-pot exhibits, although there is no rule to stipulate the way that the plant should be grown, it is more sensible – but less impressive than the 360° viewing – to grow at approximately 270° bloom formation.
- Form embraces the pot placement in these multi-pot classes. Balance in presenting them for the approval of the judges and visitors is of prime importance. All plants do not grow at the same height and balance can be obtained by means of plinths painted black, or upturned black pots on which to stand the plants. A variety of propping materials should be carried in the show kit.

Freshness

This is self-explanatory:

- There should be no signs of aging to blooms or leaves.
- Trimming of the aging edges of a bloom will severely down-point an exhibit.
- Sun scorch marks or signs of mildew (or it having been treated) on the guard petals is a major down-pointer. Any 'live' mildew will require the removal of the exhibit.
- All petals should be present.

Also note: sizes of pots, cut-bloom board sizes, size of baskets and any other specifications and instructions in the schedule must be adhered to. The variety or varieties shown have to be the same as the register listed colour.

Two pairs of hands are required for this exhibit.

societies and exhibit at one of the shows organized by the society. As well as seeing and competing against begonias grown to the highest standards, there is also the pleasure of renewing acquaintances and competing against friends with all the camaraderie and banter that goes on.

Another advantage of staging at a begonia society show is that the begonia society appoints the judges. These judges will have had a long apprenticeship as trainees alongside qualified judges. Invariably these people will be experienced growers and exhibitors and be fully aware of what standards to expect for the different classes and varieties and the effort needed to reach those standards. At a small show there is likely to be only one judge, but at larger shows there will be two or even three judges evaluating the exhibits.

Both of the begonia societies in the UK are divided into geographical areas, and most of these areas will hold an annual begonia show. There is a wide variation in the type of venue used for these area shows. Some area shows are one-day shows held in a hall at a community centre and some area shows are allocated space in large garden centres. Some area shows are incorporated as part of a larger

flower show, such as the North West of England area show which is an open competition and is part of the amateur competitor exhibits at the Southport Flower Show, held over four days in mid-August.

All types of begonias, both non-tuberous and tuberous, are exhibited at area shows. The types of exhibit for tuberous begonias are divided into four categories: cut blooms, pot plants, pendula plants and multiple planting for overall display. The schedule and number of classes for each of the area shows will vary slightly.

At an area show the highest prized class for cut blooms is likely to be 'six cut blooms of tuberous begonias, not less than three distinct varieties'. There may also be classes for three cut blooms in different colour categories: white or cream, red or crimson, yellow or orange, picotee or bicolour. There may be a class for three cut blooms of any variety or even a class for just one cut bloom. Many exhibitors will aim to put their best blooms in the 'six cut bloom' class and any blooms they have spare will be entered into the 'three cut bloom' classes. The bloom boards are always supplied by the area society.

At an area show the classes for pot plants can vary considerably between the different shows. Some shows will have a grouping of six pot plants, with no less than three distinct varieties, as the top prize. Other shows will have just a three plant group as the top prize. There may be classes for multi-stemmed plants, single-stemmed plants with side shoots, or even single-stemmed plants with no side shoots. Often the maximum size of the plant pot is specified. There may be a class for multiflora begonias or even a class for scented tuberous begonias.

There is usually only one class for pendula tuberous begonias at the area shows, although the stipulations on the schedule may vary from show to show. At some shows there will be no conditions laid down; at others the maximum size of the basket may be specified. There is no limit on the number of tubers that can be grown in the basket.

Not all of the area shows will have a class for a display of tuberous begonias. Where there is a class, the schedule will define the area of the display, what plants are to be included, and how many plants can be displayed.

For all these classes at the area shows the prize

money will be quite modest but this is of secondary importance to having taken part and possibly winning a red card. At each of the area shows in England and Wales, the National Begonia Society awards a bronze medal for the best cut bloom and a bronze medal for the best pot plant.

Anyone who has started growing tuberous begonias, or thinks they may be interested in showing tuberous begonias, is strongly recommended to go to their nearest area show and see what standards can be achieved, and perhaps talk to the exhibitors, and if not already a member, join the society. Each area show has classes for novice and intermediate growers to give special encouragement to new exhibitors who may feel they are not experienced enough to compete with experienced growers. In the novice classes there will be one class for one pot plant and one class for three cut blooms, and likewise for the intermediate classes. The definition of novice and intermediate seems to vary from area to area, but a novice may be someone who has not won more than three first prizes in any class and an intermediate someone who has not won more than five first prizes. However, once they have caught a taste for showing, most exhibitors do not stay in these categories but want to move on to the open classes to compete against the experienced growers. The details of the dates and venues for all the area shows are shown in the society bulletins and on the society websites.

Each of the UK societies also holds a national show. The national show for the Scottish Begonia Society is held as part of the three-day Ayr Flower Show in early August. The national show for the National Begonia Society is held as part of the two-day Gardeners' Weekend held at Kings Heath, Birmingham at the end of August or beginning of September. The begonia exhibits are only a small part of these shows and there are many other attractions both horticultural and non-horticultural. These shows are a great day out for the whole family.

As with the area shows, the national shows cater for all types of begonias but tuberous begonias are likely to be the majority of the exhibits. Again there are classes for pot plants, cut blooms and pendula tuberous begonias, even multifloras and species, but the main differences with the national shows are that there are far more classes, more trophies to be won, much more prize money and, more importantly, the very best growers in the country will be competing. Both shows are held in marquees, which give ideal bright conditions for viewing begonia flowers.

At both shows, the top prize for cut bloom growers is awarded for a board of twelve cut blooms of tuberous double begonias with not less than eight distinct varieties (nine distinct varieties at Ayr). The winner of this class in Scotland is declared as the British Cut Bloom Champion for the year. As well as the twelve-boards there are prizes for six-boards, three-boards of various colours and single blooms. There are prizes, trophies and rosettes for the best bloom in show and also best blooms of the individual colours. As with the area shows there are classes for novice and intermediate growers.

The top prize awarded for pot plant growers at Ayr is the Scottish Pot Plants Championship consisting of a table of nine plants in pots. At Birmingham the top prize is the British Pot Plants Championship consisting of seven plants in pots. At both shows there are classes with fewer numbers of plants, classes for plants with restricted pot size and single stems with side shoots, and in Scotland there is a class for single stem pot plants with no side shoots. The best pot plant in the show receives a prize and a trophy. There is a class for one pot plant plus one cut bloom of the same variety. One major difference separating the national shows is that in Scotland the pot plants are displayed against the side of the tent so the flowers are trained to face forward, whereas in England flowers are trained to give all-round viewing. Again there are classes for novices and intermediates at both shows.

As well as the classes for pendula begonias, there are classes for various types of display that are judged for overall effect rather than individual plants. Some of the displays consist of a mixture of tuberous and non-tuberous begonias. There are classes for species tuberous begonias and also for bedding or multiflora varieties. At both shows there are the classes for the best new seedlings, which can be cut blooms, pot plants or pendulas. These are very interesting exhibits showing the new developments from the amateur hybridizers.

At both the national shows and at some of the bigger area shows, there will be a society bureau that

POT PLANTS OR CUT BLOOMS?

At a begonia show in the United Kingdom, most exhibits for tuberous begonias are in the pot plant and cut bloom classes. The cut bloom classes were originally introduced because transporting cut blooms to a show was far easier than transporting the multi-flowering bulky pot plants. Today, however, easier transporting is not the prime reason for growing cut blooms. The cut bloom grower is looking for absolute perfection in a single bloom, which along with other perfect single blooms will make up a perfect board on the judging day at a show. The pot plant grower also is looking for a perfect plant but as well as the blooms there are other factors to consider such as the foliage, the number of blooms, the positioning of blooms and getting all the blooms in flower at the same time, so there is more of a compromise with a pot plant. There is great rivalry between the two types of growers, each claiming that their discipline requires the most skill to produce the top prize-winning exhibits, a twelve-board of cut blooms or a group of seven pot plants.

As mentioned one big advantage when showing cut blooms as opposed to pot plants is that cut blooms are very much easier to transport to the show. Pot plants can be huge and heavy and the blooms are difficult to protect during transit. If several pot plants are to be shown a large estate car will be needed to transport them or maybe hiring a van will be necessary. Also if the show lasts for more than one day it will be necessary to go back at the end of the show to retrieve the plants. Cutting and transporting cut blooms is not easy but nothing like as difficult as transporting pot plants.

Pot plants also take up far more space in the greenhouse compared with plants grown for cut blooms, which means fewer plants and varieties can be grown as pot plants and more care has to be taken in the varieties chosen. In Scotland there are classes for pot plants grown as a single stem with no side shoots. Growing this way takes up far less room and more plants and varieties can be fitted into the greenhouse.

Cut blooms are grown one bloom on one stem, and although the stem and bloom have to be supported, this is nothing like the work necessary to manipulate the stems and constantly adjust the supports for the multitude of blooms on a pot plant.

Also a cut bloom grower is only interested in the bloom, it does not matter what the foliage is like, whereas a pot plant grower may be able to get away with removing one or two disfigured leaves, but not more or the plant will be unfit for exhibition, no matter how good the flowers are.

It may seem that everything is in favour of the cut bloom grower, but there are some disadvantages and particular problems when growing cut blooms. Cut blooms are only really grown for exhibition. Unless you are a cut bloom grower, the attraction is debatable of a greenhouse full of cut blooms grown single stemmed with only one flower per plant and each flower surrounded by a nine-inch polystyrene plate.

The judges will closely examine every cut bloom on an exhibition board, so freshness, form and size are critical. Every slight blemish on a bloom will be down-pointed. Growing cut blooms, however, means just one bloom per plant and if there are any defects such as a marked boom, colour run, blotching, double centres, warts, edging or insect damage, a top grower will discard the bloom, so that is the end of the plant for that growing year. A top grower may be growing a hundred or more cut bloom plants to aim towards a satisfactory twelve-board. With a pot plant it is possible to carefully remove an odd bad bloom or two without seriously affecting the appearance of the plant.

When growing to exhibit cut blooms, timing is much more critical than if growing to exhibit pot plants. A cut bloom is at its best for perhaps two or three days depending on the variety and weather conditions. Consequently a cut bloom grower will grow several plants of the same variety, varying the stopping times, in order to get at least one bloom at peak condition for the show. Again this means more plants have to be grown. A pot plant, depending on the variety, will stay in an exhibitable condition for perhaps up to two weeks, and if care is taken it could be entered into more than one show. Pendula begonias last even longer.

If a cut bloom grower is growing for a particular major show, once the blooms are cut and taken to the show, that is the end of any colour in the greenhouse. All that is left is a mass of green single-stemmed plants. At least when growing pot plants for showing there will be a few more weeks of colour to enjoy.

Some varieties of tuberous begonias are more suited for growing as cut blooms whereas other varieties make better pot plants. Cut bloom varieties need to have big round flowers with good depth and plenty of petals and preferably a rosebud centre. For pot plant growing, the size of blooms is not as important, but a variety has to produce side shoots and flexible stems so that the stems and blooms can be manipulated into position. The plant should not be too short and should have good foliage all the way down the stems.

Analysis of the winning twelve-boards of cut blooms at the Ayr Show of the Scottish Begonia Society and the Birmingham Show of the National Begonia Society for 2000 to 2009 reveals that, excluding seedlings, sixty different varieties were exhibited. The top twenty-four in order of popularity were:

'Powder Puff': pale pink
'Nichola Coates': salmon pink
'Sweet Dreams': pink
'Beryl Rhodes': peach
'Tom Brownlee': red
'Mary Heatley': orange
'Monica Bryce': pale yellow
'Bali Hi': white/yellow picotee
'Falstaff': deep rose pink
'Roy Hartley': salmon pink
'Anniversary': orange yellow bicolour
'Mrs E. McLauchlan': pink bicolour
'Gypsy': deep salmon red
'Linda Jackson': red
'City of Ballarat': orange
'Colin Hamilton': orange
'Fiona Ramsey': pink bicolour
'Geoff Bizley': yellow
'George Tatton': orange
'Ruby Young': white picotee
'Tahiti': coral apricot
'Anne Crawford': pale yellow
'Fred Martin': cream picotee
'Helen Jessica': orange

It was interesting to see some of the differences between the varieties at the two shows. In England, 'Nichola Coates' and 'Powder Puff' were particularly popular for showing, whereas in Scotland, 'Sweet Dreams' and 'Mary Heatley' were the most favoured.

Analysis of the winning major pot plant exhibit at the Ayr Show of the Scottish Begonia Society and the Birmingham Show of the National Begonia Society for 2000–2009 shows that forty-six different varieties were exhibited. The top twenty-five in order of popularity were:

'Mrs E. McLauchlan': pink bicolour
'Sweet Dreams': pink
'Roy Hartley': salmon pink
'Powder Puff': pale pink
'Tahiti': coral apricot
'Beverley B': orange yellow bicolour
'Gay Gordon': cream picotee
'Whispers': cream
'Apricot Delight': pale apricot
'Vera Coates': orange bicolour
'Fairylight': white picotee
'Fiona Ramsey': pink bicolour
'Jessie Cruickshank': white picotee
'Jessie Wright': apricot bicolour
'Linda Jackson': red
'Sugar Candy': pink
'Beryl Rhodes': peach
'Fred Martin': cream picotee
'Angela Jane': light orange
'Beryl Spurr': cream picotee
'Billie Langdon': white
'Cancan': yellow picotee
'Emma Daisy': orange
'Jessica': orange
'Midas': yellow

Note that the varieties 'Powder Puff', 'Sweet Dreams', 'Roy Hartley' and 'Mrs E. McLauchlan' feature highly on both lists.

So what should you exhibit: pot plants or cut blooms? Perhaps the answer is to grow and exhibit some of each.

is staffed by officials for the duration of the show. The bureau is a small booth or kiosk consisting of a table often adorned with a few begonias, and a few chairs. Sometimes there are plants and auxiliary items such as plant supports for sale. The bureau acts as a meeting place for members, even a resting place sometimes, but it is primarily a place where members of the public can seek advice on growing and propagating begonias and, if sufficiently interested, can join the society. At Ayr there is an impressive display stand of begonias erected by the members of the Scottish Begonia Society.

If you are at all interested in growing or showing tuberous begonias, then try to go to one of the area or national shows. If the show lasts for more than one day, go on the first day when the begonias will be at their best, just as the judges have assessed them. Study the winning exhibits, and see if you agree with the judges. Remember size is important, especially with cut blooms, but form and freshness are more important. Make a note of the varieties that have won the prizes, talk to the exhibitors and judges and perhaps you will be inspired enough to have a go at showing the following year.

Part of the National Show at Birmingham.

CHAPTER 10

Hybridizing

A hybrid is the offspring of two plants of differing species or varieties of plants. Hybrids are created when the pollen from one kind of plant is used to fertilize the stigma of an entirely different variety, resulting in an entirely new plant.

The first begonia hybrids were produced in the 1840s and the first commercial hybrid of a flowering begonia was introduced in 1870. Since then different species and then cultivars have been hybridized leading to the named varieties of begonias grown today. Selected parents were crossed and from the seedlings produced promising plants were singled out to be grown on. If it was found to be a significant improvement, a plant could be named and propagated vegetatively by cuttings to build up a stock. Modern large, double-flowered tuberous begonias bear no resemblance to the original small single-flowered species of begonia that were first hybridized. Several new named varieties of begonias still appear every year but not many prevail for long.

The professional or serious hybridizer will decide upon a variety or colour type and consider whether there is a property that can be improved and then attempt to cross the variety with a plant that has this improvement. There has not been a begonia produced that cannot be improved. Among the properties that can be considered are bloom form (colour, size, depth, shape, type of centre, number of petals, smooth or wavy petals, picotee edging, scent), and habit of growth (height, number of side shoots, thickness and strength of stems, flexibility and the pendular habit of stems, attractiveness of foliage, ease of propagation, keeping properties). The plant to be improved can be the male or female of the cross. Out of the large number of seedlings that will be produced there is only a slight chance that one or two will have the improvement without the detriment of other properties.

For the less serious grower, hybridizing tuberous begonias can be a fascinating hobby. The chance of

Selected cuttings to be grown on for pollen.

Male flower showing the ripe anthers with pollen.

Female stigma ready for pollination.

producing a worthwhile new variety is remote (though not impossible), but the growing, anticipation and flowering of your own hybrids is very rewarding. One can never be sure what the new plants will produce.

The main difficulty with hybridizing tuberous begonias is the production of pollen. Because the begonias are fully double they do not produce pollen under normal growing conditions. To produce pollen, basal or stem cuttings are taken from the selected varieties from June onwards and rooted in 3in (7.5cm) pots containing a weak mixture such as 1:1 peat:sand. The cuttings are never fed, barely watered and grown in low light. Side shoots and flower buds are not removed. The neglected cutting is convinced that it is dying so it tries to reproduce itself. So with luck, in September single or semi-double male flowers are produced with pollen. Some varieties produce pollen more readily than others. Some varieties never seem to produce pollen.

Healthy plants with female flowers need to be available at this time to receive the pollen, so the female flowers should not have been removed as would normally be done when growing begonias for cut blooms or pot plants. Female tuberous begonia flowers are always single, have a three-winged seed pod at the base and are carried as side buds to the central male flower. The male flower is ready as soon as the pollen is available. The female flower is ready when it is fully expanded, two or three days after opening.

Pollination is best done in the middle of the day in a warm, dry atmosphere. Using a small, soft dry brush the pollen is transferred from the male anthers to the female stigma. The same pollen can be transferred to more than one female flower and more than one variety and can be repeated on different days. Before moving on to another pollen variety, brushes should be sterilized in methylated spirits and dried. All crosses should be labelled and recorded, female parent × male parent, with the date.

After a few days the petals will fall from the female flower and the seed pod will start to enlarge. It will take about six weeks for the seed pod to ripen fully. Some heating of the greenhouse may be necessary during this period. When the pods have turned brown and the outside looks dry, they can be removed from the plant. The pods must be gathered before they split open, otherwise the seed will be lost. Placed in a suitable receptacle in warm conditions the pod will split open in a few days and the seed can be collected. It is important to separate the seed from the chaff to prevent mould on storage. This can be done by placing the seed on to a sheet of white paper and tipping the paper carefully. The seed will roll off, leaving the debris behind. The seed can now be stored in a cool dry place until required for sowing.

Growing from seed is carried out as described in Chapter 2. Not all seed will be viable but from the seed that is viable there are likely to be hundreds of seedlings. These will probably be started in the

Ripe seed pod and seed.

greenhouse but then grown on outside.

When the begonias are in bloom a check should be made to see if by some lucky chance one or two plants have a particular merit. If there are any promising plants showing a distinct improvement, they should be labelled and the tubers kept for growing in the greenhouse the following year. If after that a plant is still thought to be special it should be grown for a further one or two years just to make sure that it is stable, and plenty of cuttings taken from it. Ask other growers for their opinion. At the larger begonia shows there are classes for seedlings so it may be worthwhile entering to get an expert opinion on the plant or bloom, possibly gaining a Preliminary Certificate that could eventually lead to an Award of Merit. The begonia can be named by the grower and entered on the register of the National Begonia Society.

SPORTS

A small number of named varieties of tuberous begonias were not the result of hybridization but were sports from other hybrid named varieties. A sport is part of a plant that shows a marked difference from the rest of the plant. In the case of tuberous begonias sometimes there is a different colour or different markings on a bloom that make it worthwhile to propagate, by cuttings, that part of the plant. Any sport needs to be grown for a few seasons to make sure it does not revert to its original form. The variety 'Kathryn Hartley' (pale pink) is a sport from 'Roy Hartley' (salmon pink), and the variety 'Ann Hartley' (cream) is a sport from 'Kathryn Hartley'.

CHAPTER 11

Propagation by cuttings

There are several reasons for taking cuttings in order to propagate selected begonia varieties. No matter how carefully the begonias have been grown, almost certainly over the winter dormancy period some tubers will be lost so these will need to be replaced. After a few years, tubers can become very scarred and reluctant to throw up as many shoots, so these too need to be replaced. Named varieties of tuberous begonias can be expensive, especially new varieties, so it is worthwhile increasing stock by propagation. When attempting to hybridize new improved varieties of tuberous begonias, the promising seedlings can only be propagated by taking cuttings. Taking cuttings and cultivating cutting tubers is an important part of begonia growing.

The taking and striking (rooting) of cuttings from tuberous begonias is not an exact science. Some are lost by rotting off, some do not root, some do not form a tuber. However, as one becomes more successful there is great satisfaction at the end of the year when harvesting the cutting tubers, which can be anything from the size of a pea to the size of a walnut. There is even greater satisfaction when the cutting tubers start into growth the following year.

There are many different methods of taking and striking cuttings. They can be rooted into trays, or as three or four cuttings around the edge of a pot, or potted individually into small pots. Cuttings can be rooted in peat and perlite, peat and vermiculite, or

This is a plant showing a typical basal cutting in the front of the main stem.

50 per cent multipurpose compost mixed with vermiculite, perlite or sand. They can be rooted in coir, moss from the lawn or even just rooted in water.

The cuttings that I take are normally put into individual small (1½in or 4cm diameter) plastic pots. To support the cuttings whilst rooting takes place, I use bamboo kebab sticks purchased from the local supermarket. These are thrown away after use and never used twice. I use a proprietary brand of seed and cutting compost, which is a light compost with very little fertilizer in it. I prefer to take my cuttings in the earlier half of the year. Later cuttings are harder to root. It is most important to label the cuttings as soon as they have been taken.

There are three main types of cuttings: basal cuttings, stem (axil) cuttings, and leaf cuttings.

BASAL CUTTINGS

These are the spare stems taken from the tuber, ideally when they are 2–3in (5–7.5cm) high and the width of your finger. To take a basal cutting, remove the compost from around the stem, and with the finger and thumb grip the base of the cutting and waggle it about. It should break away from the tuber. Or with a very sharp knife remove the cutting with a small sliver of tuber. If you have been lucky there may even be a few roots that come away with the cutting. Whenever a knife is used to remove any type of cutting it is advisable to dip the knife blade into methylated spirit to sterilize it, in order to lessen

The unwanted leaf and the best part of the left-hand leaf have been removed so that the cutting does not have to support any more foliage than it needs. The cutting has been planted and a kebab stick inserted to support the cutting until rooting takes place.

the risk of carrying virus or disease from one plant to another. The wound on the tuber is now brushed with sulphur to prevent rotting. Leave the soil away from the tuber for a day or two so that the break or cut can callus over; then replace the compost.

The base of the cutting taken should be lightly dusted with hormone rooting powder. This will also discourage fungal attack. I remove excess leaf so that the cutting does not have to support more foliage than it needs. The cutting is now planted in the chosen compost, gently firmed in, placed in the propagator and lightly watered. All that is required now is for the cutting to produce some roots. This should begin to occur between fourteen and thirty days. The only attention the cutting will require during this time will be a light misting and the occasional watering.

STEM (AXIL) CUTTINGS

These are the sideshoots that grow from the axil, where the leaf joins the main stem of the plant. At the axil, at the bottom of the side shoot you will always find a bract protecting the eye. This eye will grow the roots when the cutting is planted.

The removed basal cutting.

The rooted cutting.

Axil cuttings: first cut is down the side of the stem; the second cut is along the top of the leaf stem.

The cutting is taken using either a scalpel or a craft knife. Be very careful when making the cuts. The first cut is the downward cut along the plant stem. Cut until an imaginary line is reached where the top edge of the leaf stalk joins the stem. The second cut is along the top edge of the leaf stalk until it meets the cut on the stem. The axil cutting will now detach from the main plant. The axil on the main plant now needs to be dusted with green sulphur powder to prevent any rot setting in. The axil cuttings that have been taken now need to be cleaned up, by removing any unnecessary foliage, rubbing off any parts of the bract which may have come away with the cutting and dusting the cuts with a hormone rooting powder. The cutting now needs to be planted into a small pot in the chosen compost, lightly firmed in, placed in the propagator and lightly watered. A kebab stick is then pushed through an appropriate leaf to hold the cutting until rooting takes place.

Great care is required when taking axil cuttings.

Being too heavy handed with a scalpel can cause considerable damage to a plant. A safer way of getting cuttings from a side shoot is to let it grow a little bigger, and take the cutting part way along the side shoot, making the cut just underneath a bract, then treating the cutting as before. Eventually the

Three axil cuttings, ready for dusting with hormone powder and planting.

Different types of cuttings.

stub of the side shoot will fall off from the main stem causing no damage to the plant and leaving the eye to grow another side shoot from the same axil. This gives a second chance to take even more cuttings. Stem (axil) cuttings can be the main source of cuttings from a begonia plant.

LEAF CUTTINGS

The leaf with its stalk can be used as a cutting. Taking leaf cuttings has never been very popular but it can be a worthwhile method of taking a lot of cuttings. None of the methods of propagating begonias by cuttings is foolproof. There is always an element of luck as to whether the cutting will root or

A plant showing a basal cutting and two axil cuttings (top), and the same plant with the three cuttings removed (bottom). Note that the two axil cuts have been coated with green sulphur powder to prevent any rot setting in.

Leaf cutting with a good clean cut.

AFTERCARE

When the cuttings have rooted they need to be transferred into a larger pot, but now using either a John Innes No 2 soil-based compost or a suitable multipurpose compost. There is no need to pot on larger than a 1 litre (5in) pot and if the cuttings were taken in the earlier part of the year the pots can be left outside all summer, feeding two or three times with a general purpose fertilizer. In the first season

not and this is particularly so with leaf cuttings. There is nothing to lose by trying to root a few leaves. More often than not when taking other types of cuttings one or two leaves will have to be trimmed off, so instead of throwing them in the bin have a go at rooting them.

First take a leaf and ensure that the bottom cut of the stalk is nice and clean, and dust the cut with hormone rooting powder. The next step is to take a small pot and half fill it with the chosen rooting compost. Make a small hole in the compost, insert the leaf and gently firm in. Finally, push a kebab stick through the leaf to hold it in place until it has rooted and place the pot on the hot bed. Rooting is generally quicker when compared to other types of cuttings. When rooted, transfer to a larger pot.

A couple of leaf cuttings that have been potted up and are waiting for the kebab sticks to be pushed through the leaves to support them whilst rooting takes place.

The first picture demonstrates what can be achieved: a very nice rooted leaf cutting with a growing shoot right alongside the edge of the pot. When the growing shoot is large enough there is no reason why the new shoot should not be taken as a basal cutting so as to increase your stock still further. The second picture shows the new leaf cutting with the compost shaken off. The small new roots and the growing shoot are starting to form. This cutting will be re-potted and grown on.

all that is required of the cutting is to form a small tuber. To help them, once the cutting has produced seven or eight leaves, the growing tip is nipped out. By preventing the cutting from flowering, all the vigour should go to forming a new tuber. Once the growing tip has been removed, side shoots will be produced. When the shoots have three or four leaves they in turn should also be nipped out at the tips. Later in the year as the daylight hours get shorter, the callus that formed at the base of the cutting will start to swell, forming a small cutting tuber. The cuttings are brought back into the greenhouse before the start of any frosts. A temperature of at least 10°C (50°F) is needed to keep the cuttings growing, so some heating is necessary, if for only part of the greenhouse. Lower temperatures will lead to rotting of the root system and the cutting tuber. Try to keep the cuttings just about growing until Christmas, after which allow them to dry out and they will then start to die back.

Finally the cutting tubers are harvested. If the cuttings were taken correctly and looked after properly, the reward should be a mixture of assorted sizes of cutting tubers. Some will produce tiny tubers the size of a pea; others may be the size of a walnut, or even bigger, depending how lucky you have been. This is a really exciting time of the year for me: to

see a small cutting tuber from a variety that I particularly want is highly satisfying, a welcome bonus.

The cutting tubers now need a resting time. I have found the best way of keeping them in their resting period is to lay them in a tray and cover them with coir. The cutting tubers must be kept dry and free from frost for about three weeks. Any longer than this is likely to result in the smaller cutting tubers shrinking and becoming hard, and possibly rotting when planted up. The cutting tubers can now be planted up as described in Chapter 3, and the whole cycle started off once again.

If there are cuttings taken after the end of July, they need to be grown on at a temperature no less than 10°C (50°F) and watered and fed right through until the following February or March before being allowed to die back. After a week or two of resting, the cutting tubers can be started back into growth in the hot bench or propagator.

The plants from which the cuttings have been taken should not be forgotten. If stem cuttings have been taken the adult plants can look quite naked now that all the side shoots have been removed and these plants cannot be used as exhibition pot plants. However, there is no reason why these plants cannot be used to grow exhibition cut blooms. The plants have had quite a shock to their system by removing

Stripped of all side shoots, all the energy must go upwards to develop a big strong plant and produce a large bloom.

the side shoots so the plants have only one option at the present time and that is to grow upwards. They will grow thicker and taller and all their energy will be concentrated on that. In reality a plant is thinking to itself that it needs to reproduce and produce a flower and seed for survival, so by providing the plants with the necessary feeds they will be able to produce superb exhibition quality blooms. If only basal cuttings have been taken, the plants can be grown for cut blooms or as pot plants even if just one main stem with side shoots is all that remains.

The best cutting tubers are obtained from healthy plant material, typically found in vigorous two- or three-year-old plants. If an old tuber produces only weak spindly shoots, they are probably not worth taking as cuttings; perhaps the plant should be consigned to the compost heap.

Cuttings rooting nicely.

CHAPTER 12

Pests, diseases and defects

Fortunately there are very few pest and disease problems with begonias and the few problems that do exist are easily treated if spotted in the early stages. It is important, however, that if you find an infestation of tarsonemid mite or eelworm, or an outbreak of mildew, plants and tubers must not be passed on to other growers, nor should any plant material be taken to exhibit at flower shows, until the problem has been treated and eliminated.

The plant defects described are usually minor and the flower defects are only of real concern to serious exhibitors.

PESTS

Several pests are mentioned here but the only two really serious pests of tuberous begonias are vine weevil and tarsonemid mite. Protection against vine weevil grubs is essential or there will certainly be tuber losses. Tarsonemid mite is not very common but an outbreak can devastate a greenhouse full of tuberous begonias.

Vine weevil

Otiorhynchus sulcatus, better known as the vine weevil, is the scourge of all begonia growers. The damage they can cause is unbelievable. The adult weevil is a beetle-like insect about half an inch in

The adult vine weevil.

Vine weevil grubs and a newly hatched adult. The colour of the adult will change to a brownish grey as it matures.

length and brownish grey in colour. It moves very slowly and is pretty well armoured. From July onwards it is quite common to see them climbing up walls both inside and outside the greenhouse. You can generally tell when one is about because it chews large holes in the edges of leaves. The adult vine weevils are all female and do not require a mate to produce eggs. In June, July and August these creatures are on the move and they lay their eggs either on or just under the surface of the compost adjacent to a begonia stem. You will not be aware of the eggs as they are very small but you will be aware of the damage once the eggs have hatched and the resulting grubs have been to work. When the eggs have hatched you will still not be aware that anything is amiss, but underneath the compost the small vine weevil grubs are hard at work eating the roots and burrowing into the tubers. The larvae are creamy white in colour with a brownish black head, growing to about ½in (12mm) long, and are not unlike a maggot to look at. If they are not checked they will tunnel into the tubers and eat the tuber from the inside out, creating a maze of tunnels, and the tuber will be of no further use to anyone. The grub will eventually turn into an adult vine weevil, and unless stopped will wander off and start the whole process again next season.

Vine weevils are more of a problem now than in the past. It is thought that the widespread use of peat-based compost and the increased importation of plants from the continent are the reasons.

One way to get round the problem is to buy compost that has been pre-treated by the manufacturer with imidacloprid or chlorpyrifos. The compost is more expensive but will solve the vine weevil problem. These chemicals are not available to amateur growers.

Fortunately there are now products available to the amateur on the market, containing imidacloprid or thiacloprid, which are very effective for killing vine weevils. They are systemic insecticides that will give protection for up to six months. The products are diluted and watered into the compost. Provided the instructions have been followed properly there should not be any further problems with this destructive pest.

One other method is by biological control. Parasitic nematodes, specifically effective against vine weevil, can be purchased to water into the compost and these will protect for the whole season.

Tarsonemid mite

An attack of tarsonemid mite is probably what begonia growers dread most. Tarsonemid mite has the potential to destroy all the plants in the green-

Vine weevil damage to a tuber.

Corky tracking on the stems, distorted leaves and brown scaling under the leaves are a sure sign of tarsonemid mite.

This is what tarsonemid mite does to the flower.

house if not spotted early, affecting the whole crop within days.

The mite itself is very small: it cannot be seen with the naked eye. Usually the first sign of tarsonemid mite attack is a corky-looking track mark on the stem or leaf stem. If this is seen, then look closely at the growing tips, as the mites tend to feed on them. If the tips and leaves are showing distortion and are misshapen, remove any affected plants immediately from the greenhouse and isolate them. To avoid losing the plants, treatment must be started as soon as possible.

There are chemicals that will kill the tarsonemid mite but these are not available for amateur use. The only control available to the amateur begonia grower is the biological control *Amblyseius cucumeris*. *Amblyseius cucumeris* is a mite itself, just about visible to the naked eye, and will feed on the tarsonemid mites and also any thrips. The *Amblyseius cucumeris* is available in slow release sachets, which are effective for six to eight weeks. If the sachets are placed around any affected plants, the tarsonemid mites will be killed and the new growth on the begonia will grow clean.

Many begonia exhibitors, who grow more than a few plants, use *Amblyseius cucumeris* sachets as a precaution to prevent any attack from tarsonemid mite. The sachets have a small hanging hook attached. The bags are pierced and hung every six

feet or so along the length of the greenhouse on convenient leaves. Providing they are used as the weather is getting warmer, say, early June and maybe again in the middle of August, the stock of begonias will be protected. Weighing the cost of named variety begonia tubers against the reasonable cost of a few packets of predators, it seems a worthwhile investment. The predatory mites are so tiny that exhibitors need have no worries about them being seen on any plants that are shown.

Apart from the *Amblyseius cucumeris*, there are several ways to avoid getting an attack of tarsonemid mite in the first place:

- Try to avoid the dry arid conditions that the mite thrives in. Make sure the plants are correctly watered and not allowed to dry out for any length of time.
- Make sure there is adequate ventilation, as the mites do not like cool, damp conditions. Perhaps the warmer weather there has been in recent years is the reason for the increase in infestations that seem to be occurring.
- When new stock is acquired it should be isolated for a couple of months and only added to the greenhouse if it looks healthy.

Caterpillars

Caterpillars of the tortrix moth can cause problems with begonias by eating holes in the foliage and buds. The caterpillars are coloured green and are not easy to spot amongst the foliage. Netting of windows, vents and doors will prevent the moth from entering the greenhouse and laying eggs on the leaves. The imidacloprid- or thiacloprid-based vine weevil killers are also effective against caterpillars.

Eelworm

Most begonia growers will never come across an eelworm attack. Eelworm is not a problem nowadays, possibly because begonias are now grown almost universally in sterilized compost in plastic pots. Years ago many growers used 'molehills' collected from the fields, often fertilized with dried sheep manure, and planted in difficult-to-sterilize clay pots; perhaps this is the reason why problems with eelworm were more prevalent then.

The hot water treatment for tubers was originally developed to kill eelworm and prevent any carry over from one season to the next. The treatment involves immersing the tubers in hot water at a temperature of 115°F (46°C) for a period of 15–20 minutes. The tubers are then removed and plunged into cold water for a further 15 minutes. Some growers perform the hot water treatment after harvesting the tubers but before the tubers are stored for the winter. Other growers will do the hot water treatment after winter storage but just before the tubers are planted out. Many begonia growers still carry out the hot water treatment, even though it may not be necessary for the control of eelworm, because it is thought that soaking in the hot water encourages more shoots to appear when the tuber starts into growth.

There are two types of eelworm that attack tuberous begonias. Leaf eelworm (as its name suggests) starts off by attacking the leaves. If an area on a leaf between the leaf veins turns brown, then leaf eelworm must be suspected, and the plant should immediately be isolated from the rest of the stock. Leaf eelworm is easily spread so the remaining stock needs to be checked very carefully. If the brown leaf area on the isolated plant turns black and other leaves start to show similar brown areas between leaf veins, this is almost certainly leaf eelworm and the plant and tuber should be destroyed. It would die anyway. There is no treatment available to the amateur grower, although it has been reported that heat treatment of the whole plant will kill leaf eelworm.

The other eelworm that can attack tuberous begonias is the root-knot eelworm. This nematode attacks the roots causing swellings on both the roots and the tubers. An attack by root-knot eelworm results in stunted growth, yellowing of leaves, wilting and eventual death due to the inability of the roots to absorb water and nutrients. If the tuber is examined it will be found to be covered in galls or swellings. Fortunately root-knot eelworm is even more rare than leaf eelworm. Some growers add powdered mothballs to their compost as a deterrent. There is no cure available to the amateur and any plants showing symptoms should be destroyed.

Even though eelworm is rarely come across these days, it is still prudent to isolate any new stock for a few weeks to make sure there are no problems before adding to the greenhouse. A remote quarantine area is a worthwhile provision.

Sciarid fly

Sciarid flies, also known as fungus gnats or mushroom flies, are the little black flies that are quite often seen running and flying on the surface of pots and heated beds particularly if they contain peat or peat-based composts. If there is only the odd one or two it is not a problem. However, if there are a lot of them they can become a nuisance and start to cause damage. The sciarid flies lay their eggs in the compost; these hatch into tiny white worms growing to about ¼in (6mm) long, and live mainly on decaying matter in the compost. If you find a cutting that has not rooted and started to rot, look carefully and these worms will probably be seen. Often with bad cases of stem rot these worms will be seen eating the rotten plant material. Strangely these flies are not often seen living in soil based composts.

These flies and the worms can be got rid of by spraying or watering the compost with an insecticide containing malathion or permethrin. The imidacloprid- or thiacloprid-based vine weevil killers are also effective against sciarid fly.

Thrips

Thrips, also known as thunder flies, are very tiny narrow-bodied flies. Out in the garden they do not pose much of a problem, but if they become established in a greenhouse they become problematic. The pests suck sap from the top surface of the leaves and also flowers. Flecks of a pale whitish yellow colour are found on the leaves or flower petals. The adult flies move from plant to plant laying eggs, which hatch into young that also continue to feed on the leaves and flowers.

Control of thrips is not difficult. There are several effective insecticides that can be sprayed over the foliage. Blue sticky thrip papers can be hung at intervals throughout the greenhouse. The imidacloprid- or thiacloprid-based vine weevil killers are also effective against thrips. *Amblyseius cucumeris* mite will kill thrips as well as tarsonemid mites.

Earwigs

Earwigs are sometimes troublesome. They nibble on both leaves and flowers and commonly hide in the centre of flowers. If one is found in the centre of a bloom it can be carefully removed with a pair of tweezers.

Aphids

Aphids, or greenfly, are rarely a problem with tuberous begonias. They can occasionally be found on flower buds and new growth. They can easily be removed by using one of the many insecticide sprays that are available at most garden centres. The imidacloprid- or thiacloprid-based vine weevil killer will also eliminate greenfly.

DISEASES

Not many diseases affect tuberous begonias. Most begonia growers will have some experience of all the diseases described. Mildew and stem rot often occur at the end of the growing season and at that time are usually not a serious problem. One or two tubers showing some rot over the dormant period is almost to be expected. Powdery mildew, however, even if only slight, can be a serious problem to an exhibitor if it attacks at the wrong time and treatment to prevent an attack is better than treatment after an attack.

Powdery mildew

Powdery mildew is a fungal growth, which is more common now than in the past. The reason why is not known. It appears from nowhere, the first signs being a few grey-white spots appearing on one or two leaves of just one plant. If this is not treated, within days the spots will become widespread on the leaves and stems, and other plants will be affected. As an attack worsens, the leaves will drop off and the plants will wither and die.

A well-ventilated greenhouse with a constant movement of air will help to prevent an attack of mildew, as will avoiding overcrowding. There are a number of growers who believe that mildew can be brought on by stress and it is particularly important that plants are watered correctly: if a plant is allowed to dry out it this makes it more susceptible. Weak

An attack of mildew.

growing plants and exhausted plants at the end of the growing season are especially prone to mildew attack. White and yellow flowered begonias seem particularly prone to attack. Excessive amounts of nitrogen feed makes leaves and stem cells grow bigger, but the cell walls become thinner, the plant becomes fleshy and more readily attacked by the fungus.

When the first signs of mildew are noticed, it is fairly easy to kill and stop any spread of the disease. If only one or two plants are affected, a cotton bud dipped in a fungicide can be dabbed on the individual mildew spots. This neat fungicide will probably burn the leaves but this will not matter if it is late in the season. Alternatively, or if the mildew is more widespread, a thorough spraying of affected and unaffected plants with a systemic fungicide such as myclobutanil solution, diluted as recommended, will not burn the leaves. If the mildew is persistent, then the spraying may need to be repeated or perhaps a different fungicide used.

Multiflora begonias, especially the variety 'Le Flamboyant', are particularly prone to mildew attack. They should never be allowed to dry out at any time, and if mildew is seen they should be sprayed with a fungicide solution as soon as possible.

Many growers will spray with a fungicide at intervals throughout the growing season as a preventative against a mildew attack, starting in April and spraying monthly until the buds are selected for flowering. Spraying can start again from September onwards.

For the more serious grower, as a mildew preventative there is an electric sulphur burner available. This works by heating the sulphur to a temperature at which it will sublime and be diffused throughout the greenhouse. Using it for about four hours per night, two or three nights a week, should protect begonias from an attack of mildew.

Stem rot

Stem rot is a condition that is not usually seen until the later part of the growing season. Stem rot starts with some slight discolouration and a little bit of white fungus growth on the stem. If not spotted and treated, the rot spreads quite quickly, eventually right through the stem and the plant collapses. If the rot is near the base of the stem, the rot can travel down into the tuber, causing it to die.

If the rot is spotted early enough, the rotting area can be rubbed hard down to clean tissue, or the bad tissue can be cut away with a sharp knife. The wound is then sterilized with methylated spirit and when dry dusted with sulphur. The plant needs to be checked regularly over the next week or so to make sure the problem has been fully eradicated.

Stem rot often occurs at the back of the plant where it can lie unnoticed. It may be that when the stem rot is noticed for the first time the stem of the plant has been almost completely eaten away over a length of a couple of inches, leaving just part of the

Stem rot from a damaged leaf.

outside skin of the plant intact. When the damage is this bad, the sensible thing to do is to try to save the tuber. A sloping cut is made right through the stem underneath the stem rot damage. The cut is dried and dusted with flowers of sulphur, and hopefully the stem rot has occurred high enough up the stem so that the tuber is not harmed.

Stem rot is often started off by carelessness, such as catching the stem with the watering can, or tying the plant to the support cane too tightly so the string or twine cuts into the stem, or tying too slackly so the plant moves about and the stem chafes against the string or twine. The type of string or twine used as a tie is quite important. It should be made of a synthetic material such as polypropylene. Natural materials such as jute, sisal or raffia tend to hold water, staying wet against the stem, and are more likely to cause stem rot. A broad tie such as synthetic raffia is much less likely to cut into a stem. Falling leaves or petals left to rest against the stem will also cause stem rot. When bending a leaf, to give a bloom more light, it can be quite easily broken off. If the break is too near the stem, it allows the rot to develop. It is better to take a pair of scissors and cut off the offending leaf and then squeeze the end of the stem. All of these predicaments can and should be prevented by taking more care. Excessive nitrogen feed will also make the stem cells more liable to stem rot.

With regard to stem rot, the most important thing is to check the plants regularly and treat as soon as any is found. Giving plants plenty of space for better air circulation will help to prevent stem rot and also make it easier to spot earlier.

Tuber rot

Tuber rot here means the rotting of tubers, which can occur during the winter storage period. Tubers are actually swollen stems, so the appearance of tuber rot and the treatment is very similar to stem rot.

It is very important to check begonia tubers two or three times during the winter storage so that if there is any tuber rot occurring it can be spotted and treated early. If tuber rot is not treated early enough the whole tuber will succumb and die. Tuber rot is not always easy to spot. Sometimes there will be some white mould, sometimes there will a little damp patch, and sometimes a patch of dry skin will seem loose. A quick scrape with the fingernail will soon tell whether there is rot underneath. A rotten portion of tuber will be softish, pale grey with grey/brown streaks running through it, compared to live tuber which will be firm and pale cream coloured. Sometimes the rotten portion is quite moist, sometimes quite dry, sometimes dark brown. The treatment is the same in all cases: all the rot must be cut out and the sound part of the tuber dusted with flowers of sulphur.

There are several reasons why tuber rot might occur. The tubers may not have been dried off enough before going into storage, or the callus may not have been properly removed (*see* Chapter 3). The tubers may get damp during storage. Excessive nitrogen feeding, as with leaves and stems, will make the tubers more susceptible to rot. This is why feeding with nitrogen should not continue beyond half way through the growing season, and why high potash is fed towards the end of the season to harden off the tubers as they start to swell. Rot can spread from one tuber to another, so if possible the tubers should be separated during storage. Small cutting tubers do not seem as prone to rotting as larger adult tubers.

DEFECTS

The plant defects described here are only experienced occasionally and are not serious. The bloom defects described are mainly of interest to the cut bloom grower who is seeking absolute perfection.

Discoloured leaves

Variation in the green colour of leaves is probably due to the large variations in temperature during the early part of the growing season causing variation in the rate of growth. Later growth is usually a more uniform green colour. Discoloured leaves are no problem to the cut bloom exhibitor but can be a nuisance to the pot plant exhibitor.

Yellow leaves

If a yellow leaf occurs in the spring it can be due to a deficiency of nitrogen. A feed of high nitrogen fertilizer will rectify the problem for the rest of the leaf growth. If the yellow leaf is a large bottom leaf

and the condition is not noticed quickly, the leaf will probably be lost. It is important that in the early part of the growing season, foliar feeding is started before the plants are in their final pots when the main feeding programme can begin. Foliar feeding should be done on a dull day (*see* scorching, below). Over-watering will wash out nutrients through the bottom of the plant pot and this can result in yellow leaves. Usually the next time that yellow leaves will be seen is at the end of the season, when the plants are dying back and preparing for dormancy, which is perfectly normal.

Stunted growth

Stunted growth or slow growth, compared with other plants, is almost always due to poor root growth. Changing the compost, which may be sour, can help. If not, take the cuttings off the plant and discard the tuber.

Bud drop

Bud drop or flower drop can occur when the atmospheric conditions the plants are growing in are not right for the plants. Dry, arid conditions can be the cause, as can badly over-watering. If the greenhouse is well ventilated, the plants are watered correctly and if, when the temperatures are very hot, the greenhouse floor is damped down to create a humid atmosphere, there should be no trouble with bud drop. There is a micro-climate within the greenhouse which has to be balanced and maintained.

Leaf scorch

Tuberous begonias have soft leaves, so strong sunshine through glass, giving high temperatures, is certain to cause leaf scorch. Any water spilled on the leaves while watering will make the problem worse because each droplet acts as a magnifying glass. Watering and foliar feeding should not be carried out in strong sunshine.

It is important to apply shading to the greenhouse in April before the full heat of summer. This cools the greenhouse and diffuses the strong sunlight. Strong sunlight will cause scorching through an open roof light, so shading is also needed over the vents. The shading can be removed in October.

Begonias planted outside are less prone to leaf scorch because temperatures are lower than in the

The effect of too much sunlight.

Typical example of a tunnel centre.

greenhouse, but they will still get leaf scorch if strong sunshine falls on wet leaves.

An odd leaf with scorch is no problem to the cut bloom exhibitor. With a pot plant exhibitor it is usually possible to remove an odd scorched leaf without detriment to the plant.

Double centres

This is a bloom defect. As the name suggests the blooms have a double centre, although sometimes it

Double centre spoiling a good bloom.

is not very obvious. Some growers think that over-feeding causes double centres but other growers dispute this. A double centre would be down-pointed in a cut bloom competition, but is not quite as serious in a pot plant competition. With basket begonias it does not matter at all.

Just because one bloom has a double centre, it does not mean that other blooms on the plant will also have double centres, and quite likely the plant in the following year will not have the defect. Sometimes a bloom can have a triple centre, or even more centres.

Tunnel centres

Some varieties will open up all the petals in the centre, just leaving a hole, before the bloom has reached its full size and potential. This empty centre is called a tunnel centre and would be severely down-pointed on a show bench.

There are several varieties that are likely to give tunnel centres, such as 'Anne Crawford' (pale yellow), 'Christina Barclay' (white picotee), and 'Coppelia' (white picotee). It does not mean that these varieties should not be grown and shown, but that varieties such as these should be exhibited just before they reach full size while their centres are still intact. It does mean, however, that the size of these blooms may be slightly smaller. Tunnel centres are more likely to occur when the bloom is grown on a cutting tuber and less likely when grown on an adult tuber.

Tahiti showing a white centre.

White centres

With one or two begonia varieties, such as 'Tahiti' (coral orange) and 'Falstaff' (deep rose pink), the blooms have a tendency to grow white in the centre. To prevent this, the plants should be given more light with the blooms turned towards the side glass of the greenhouse.

Edging

This is another bloom defect. All blooms will start edging when the flowers have matured and gone past their best, but it is a fault that should not be seen on the show bench and it will be down-pointed by

the judges in cut blooms, pot plants and pendula begonias. The judges like to see fresh blooms on the show bench. Edging is a sign that the bloom is just over the top and is starting to die. It is possible to nip off a little bit of edging with nail clippers but a good judge will surely spot this.

Edging can also occur when water, which normally transpires through the bloom petals, cannot evaporate into the atmosphere and little droplets of water gather on the edge of the petals, which will start to decay. This can occur when the nights are cool, especially later on in the growing season.

The best time for watering begonias in the greenhouse is early morning; most plants do not appreciate wet feet overnight.

Colour run

Colour run is a particular problem with picotee begonia blooms where the picotee edging seems to bleed or run towards the centre of the flower. Bicolour begonias can also show this sort of problem. Colour run in a begonia bloom would be severely down-pointed on the show bench.

It is not known with certainty why colour run

Severe colour run.

Edging on a begonia that is past its best.

happens. There could be more than one reason. Variation in the amount of light, or temperatures, or overfeeding causing growth to slow down and speed up while the bloom is developing, have all been suggested as reasons for colour run.

Certain varieties are more prone to colour run and some growing seasons seem worse than others. If a variety in the greenhouse shows colour run, try moving the plant to a different area, perhaps with more light or perhaps with less light and see if the next bloom shows an improvement. Try and get another tuber of the same variety from a different source and see if this is any better. If colour run still persists perhaps it is better to stop growing that particular variety. There are plenty other picotee and bicolour varieties available.

Blotching

Blotching on begonia blooms in many ways is like colour run. Whereas colour run is a breakdown of the coloured edge on a picotee, blotching is a breakdown of uniformity on a self-coloured bloom. It often appears like thumbprints of darker colour on a paler coloured background, or vice versa (paler colour on a darker background). Any blotching of blooms on a show bench would be severely downpointed. Some bicolour varieties of begonia sometimes appear to be blotched, but this is the actual appearance of the variety, for example the variety 'Joyce Mihulka' (pale pink/dark pink bicolour).

Like colour run it is thought that variation in the amount of light, or temperatures, or overfeeding, which can slow down and speed up growth whilst the bloom is developing in the bud, may be reasons for blotching.

Begonias with orange or pink blooms seem to be the worst for blotching. Two varieties, 'Falstaff' (rose pink) and 'City of Ballarat' (bright orange) will often show blotching, whereas some other pink and orange varieties are more resistant.

Like colour run, some years are worse than others and it is worthwhile moving plants around in the greenhouse to see if this can cure the blotching. Getting another strain of the same variety from another grower may solve the problem. There is some thought that old tubers are worse for giving blotched blooms.

A wart hidden amongst the petals.

Warts

Warts are growths that are hidden between the petals, generally towards the back of a bloom. Looking from the front of the bloom, a wart will not usually be seen, but sideways on it will be visible and a show judge will certainly spot it and down-point the bloom.

It is not known what causes warts. Possibly they are under-developed petals, or possibly it is the double male flower trying to grow stamens and pollen. Fortunately warts are not very common, except that one or two varieties seem to nearly always have warts. The varieties 'Full Moon' (pale cream) and 'Linda Jackson' (bright red) often have warts in the blooms. If they can be grown wart free they are excellent varieties for the show bench. With a scalpel, a steady hand and some tweezers it is possible to remove a wart, but it is not easy.

Funnel petals, under-developed petals

These are abnormalities in a bloom, which can occur from time to time. A funnel petal is when perhaps just one petal twists and folds in on itself forming a little cone or funnel. Under developed petals are very tiny petals that started to grow normally but then aborted. Both are classified as faults, but not as serious as some of the other defects

Occasionally everything goes wrong!

A severe case of phyllody.

that have been described. With extreme care it is possible to remove a funnel petal with a pair of tweezers.

Foliar petal, phyllody

Phyllody or foliar petal is when part of a flower develops into a leaf. It is found to be most frequent on yellow varieties of begonia, also occasionally on white, cream and picotees but seldom on strong coloured varieties. Usually only the first flower produced by a plant would show phyllody, and as the first buds are generally removed, when growing begonias in the greenhouse, phyllody is not seen very often. If phyllody or foliar petal is found, the flower must be taken off the plant and in all probability the next flower will be fine. Phyllody can occur with all types of flowering tuberous begonias, and is often seen on bedding begonias.

APPENDIX

The begonia year

This is a monthly list of the tasks that need to be done when growing tuberous begonias, based on what I do at my greenhouse in south-east Lancashire at 130m above sea level. This list should be treated only as a rough guide: other growers will do some things differently and timings may need to be adjusted for other parts of the UK.

JANUARY

- Early cuttings taken last year will be dying back; remove from pots and store.
- Check adult tubers, cut out and treat with sulphur if there is any rot.
- Clean and sterilize the greenhouse.
- Wash plant pots for the coming season.
- Order plant plugs and plantlets for use in the garden.
- Sow seed crosses from last year.
- Sow purchased seed.
- Towards the end of the month, start pendula tubers.

FEBRUARY

- Finish planting any late pendulas.
- Plant adult tubers for growing into pot plants.
- Start off the cutting tubers from cuttings taken last year.
- Plant adult tubers for cut blooms for the July shows.
- Named variety tubers that have been ordered should arrive.

MARCH

- Started pendula tubers can be moved into baskets.
- Plant the remaining adult tubers after soaking in tepid water.
- Prick out seedlings when size allows.
- Buy begonia tubers from garden centres for outside use.

APRIL

- Pot up started cutting tubers.
- Pot up started adult tubers.
- First basal cuttings can be taken.
- Apply greenhouse shading.
- Spray all plants with leaves with a fungicide to prevent mildew.
- Plugs and plantlets will arrive, pot up and keep in the greenhouse for the time being.
- Pendulas for showing will require their first stop.

MAY

- Continue potting on cutting and adult tubers.
- Continue to take cuttings.
- Add support canes for pot plants.
- Start feeding baskets.
- Pot on the seedlings from last year crosses into 1 litre (5in) pots ready for flowering and harden off, if they are to go outside.
- Start foliar feeding.
- Remove any greenhouse insulation.
- Ventilate whenever the temperature will allow. Watch out for frost warnings and cover with fleece if necessary.

- Harden off bedding begonias, surplus cutting tubers and pendulas that are to go outside and remove early flowers.
- Pendulas for showing will require their second stop.

JUNE

- Adult cut bloom tubers in their final pots will now require staking.
- Treat pots and baskets with imidacloprid or thiacloprid to prevent vine weevil attack.
- Plant out multifloras, Non Stops and surplus tubers into the garden.
- Baskets not for show can be moved outside.
- Showmen check for show entry dates. Obtain schedules and send entry forms to shows.
- Start feeding cut blooms and pot plants with high nitrogen fertilizer.
- Ventilation should now be continuous. Vents and doors to be left open with a mesh screen in place.
- Spray again with fungicide to keep mildew at bay.
- Continue to take and root cuttings. Late cuttings can be used to produce pollen for hybridization later.
- Secure cut bloom buds and nip out growing tips for the early shows.

JULY

- The first begonia flower shows start this month.
- Secure cut bloom buds and nip out growing tips for the later shows.
- Change feed from high nitrogen to high potash for pots and baskets.
- Place polystyrene backing plates on selected buds on cut blooms.
- Remove the two small flower buds from either side of the chosen cut bloom bud when size permits.
- Remove the side buds from the male blooms on pot plants.
- Remove all growing tips from main stems and side shoots of pot plants.

- Check bloom supports and insert into pot plants.
- If showing, now is the time to check bloom boxes, Dacron, polystyrene cups, etc.

AUGUST

- The height of the flowering season for tuberous begonias in the UK and the main month for begonia flower shows.
- Exhibitors will be busy making final touches to blooms, plants and baskets ready for the shows.
- Cuttings taken this month and later will have to be grown through the winter.
- Hybrid seedlings planted in January can now be assessed.
- Decide what varieties need to be kept for the following year and what varieties can be discarded.

SEPTEMBER

- Last begonia shows early in the month.
- Cut down on the watering and stop feeding adult cut bloom and pot plant tubers.
- Feed all plants a teaspoonful of sulphate of potash, and water in.
- Early cuttings that were placed outside should now be brought back inside the greenhouse.

OCTOBER

- Stop watering adult plants and baskets.
- Cuttings should be kept watered and growing in a temperature of at least $10°C$ ($50°F$).
- Take shading off the greenhouse.
- Put insulation on the greenhouse if required.
- Order named varieties of tubers for delivery next year.
- Hybridization crosses can now commence.
- Bring back inside the greenhouse all the bedding begonias, pendulas, and large doubles that are to be kept for next year before the severe frosts.
- The greenhouse will be filling up: spray with a fungicide to prevent mildew.

- Remove any fallen leaves to avoid botrytis, check daily.
- Treat any stem rot with sulphur.

NOVEMBER

- As die-back starts and stem segments fall, remove canes and plant ties.
- When stems on the adult plants drop off, remove tubers from the pots and baskets along with some of the root ball.
- A few days later remove the last of the compost and lightly brush the tubers clean.
- About ten days later remove the calluses and dust with sulphur.
- Treat bedding begonias that are to be kept in the same way.

- Make sure the greenhouse heating is ready and frost protection fleece is handy should it be needed.
- Order seed from seed catalogues.

DECEMBER

- Hot water or bleach treat all adult tubers before storing in a frost-free environment.
- Gradually reduce watering of the cutting tubers to allow them to go into dormancy.
- Collect and clean seed from hybrid crosses.
- Send subscription for next year's Begonia Society membership.
- Review the growing year, check and amend notes taken.

Useful addresses

COMMERCIAL NURSERIES

United Kingdom

Blackmore & Langdon, Stanton Nurseries, Pensford,
Bristol BS39 4JL
Tel: 01275 332300
Email: plants@blackmore-langdon.com
www.blackmore-langdon.com

Bellcross Nurseries, Howden, Goole, East Yorkshire
DN14 7TQ
Tel: 01430 430284

Fibrex Nurseries Ltd, Honeybourne Road, Pebworth,
Warwickshire CV37 8XP
Tel: 01789 720788
www.fibrex.co.uk

USA

Antonelli Bros. Begonia Gardens, 2545 Capitola Road,
Santa Cruz, California. 95062
Tel: (408) 475-5222
www.antonellibegonias.com

Carmel Valley Begonia Gardens, 9220 Carmel Valley
Road, Carmel Valley, California. 93924
Tel: (408) 624-7231

Weidners' Begonia Gardens, 695 Normandy Road,
Encinitas, California. 92024
Tel: (619) 436-5326
www.weidners.com

White Flower Farm, Inc., P.O. Box 50, Route 63,
Litchfield, Connecticut 06759
Tel: (800) 503-9624
www.whiteflowerfarm.com

Australia

Australian Begonia Company, PO Box 915, Erica,
Victoria VIC 3825
www.candybell.com.au

COMPOSTS

Keith Singleton, Seaview Nurseries, Egremont,
Cumbria CA22 2UQ
Tel: 01946 824091

Cuttings Compost (mail order), Compost Technology
Ltd, Trewern,
Welshpool SY21 8EA
Tel: 0845 4631234
www.compost-technology.co.uk

FERTILIZERS AND SUNDRIES

Garden Direct (the mail order division of Chempak),
Hillgrove Business Park, Nazeing, Essex EN9 2BB
Tel: 01992 890550
Email: gardendirect@chempak.co.uk

N.A. Kay's Horticultural Products, Unit 10, Sneckyeat
Industrial Estate
Hensingham, Whitehaven, Cumbria CA28 8PF
Tel: 01946 692134/692135
Sunday order line number: 07903 998110
www.kaysdiscountgarden.co.uk

Two Wests and Elliot (greenhouse and gardening catalogue), Freepost YO 446, York YO30 4ZZ
Tel: 01904 696 900
www.twowests.co.uk

Nutrimate Ltd, The Power House, Lancashire Business
Park, Centurion Way, Leyland PR 26 6TZ
Tel: 01772 641181
Fax: 01772 641178

MG Electrical Ltd (Envirolite ventilated reflectors and lamps), The Warehouse, Mill Street, Scarborough YO11 1SZ
Tel: 01723 341334
Fax: 01723 341494
www.envirolites.co.uk

Parwin Heaters UK Ltd, 21 High Haden Road, Glatton Huntingdon PE28 5RU
Tel: 01487 834630
Mobile: 07889 163421
paul@metalspec.freeserve.co.uk

Knowle Nets Ltd, East Road, Bridport, Dorset DT6 4NX
Tel: 01308 424342
Fax: 01308 458186
Email: sales@knowlenets.co.uk

Panda Sticks (strong rot-proof glass fibre plant supports)
Unit 9, Network Centre
Concorde Way
Millennium Business Park
Mansfield NG19 7JZ
Tel: 01623 412340
Website: www.ericthepanda.co.uk

Scarletts, The Glasshouses, Fletching Common, Newick, Lewes, East Sussex BN8 4JJ
Tel: 0845 0945499
www.ladybirdplantcare.co.uk

Bayer Garden, Provado, 230, Cambridge Science Park, Milton Road, Cambridge CB4 OWB
Advisory line: 0845 345 4100
www.bayergarden.co.uk

Hotbox Sulphume, Hotbox International Ltd, Wallingfen Park, 223 Main Road, Newport, Brough, East Yorkshire HU15 2RH
Tel: 01430 449440
Email: sales@hotboxworld.com
www.hotboxworld.com

BEGONIA SOCIETIES

United Kingdom

The National Begonia Society
Alan Harris (Secretary), 7 Babraham Road, Sawston, Cambridge CB2 4DQ

Tel: 01223 83402
Email: alanharris329@aol.com
www.national-begonia-society.co.uk

The Scottish Begonia Society
Cathy and Allan Walkinshaw (Secretaries), 15 Hayward Avenue, Carluke NL8 4LQ
Tel: 01555 820644.
www.scottishbegoniasociety.co.uk

The South West of Scotland Begonia Society
Brenda McBurnie (Secretary), Masonhill, Ayr KA7 3NU
Tel: 01292 284673
Email: swsbegsociety@aol.com

East of Scotland Begonia Society
May Southerland (Secretary), 4 Holly Crescent, Dunfermline KY11 8BT
Tele:01383 727874
Email: dmsfife@aol.com
www.eosbegonias.force9.co.uk

USA

American Begonia Society
Paul Rothstein, 33 Kintyre Lane, Bella Vista, AR 72715
www.begonia.org

Australia

Association of Australian Begonia Societies Inc.
Neil Connery (Secretary), PO Box 1987, Mandurah 6210, Western Australia
Tel: (08) 9582 7738
Email: neil.connery@live.com.au

New Zealand

Canterbury Begonia Circle
Mike Stevens, 47 Burnside Crescent, Christchurch 8005.

Canada

BC Fuchsia & Begonia Society
c/o Diane Rudd, #17-910 Fort Fraser Rise, Port Coquitlam BC V3C 6K3

Index of named varieties

General index

Other Gardening Books from Crowood